Praise for *Animal Communication Made Easy*

'When we don't know something we often fear or, perhaps worse, criticize and undermine it. Pea impressed me from the outset with animal communication by confirming that she doesn't have all the answers. This same philosophy was how I grew up with the bears – and to this day our team and I don't have all the answers, but connect with them in the desire to learn and be what they need us to be.

Through Pea's understanding, talent and patience, animals that are rarely given the benefit of the doubt in our often blinkered minds, are now listened to and increasingly understood. Pea takes us into the inspirational world of animal cognizance and spiritual honouring and we owe her our gratitude for helping us to communicate, understand, respect and revere all creatures – great and small – whose extraordinary world we share.

As Pea asks: "Has your intuition crawled into a cave?" Yes I think it has and we must be brave enough now to crawl back into the light.'

Jill Robinson, MBE, Dr med vet hc, Hon LLD,
Founder and CEO, Animals Asia Foundation

'Whether you live in the city with your adorable pets, or in the wild with prides of lions as I do, this delightful heart-warming book makes it clear that interspecies communication is really obvious and simple, because it's totally natural.

The mind thinks but the heart knows, so this technique is about connecting heart-to-heart.

In my vision of the future, all leaders will have mastered this subtle art, not only by speaking to the other inhabitants of this planet, but by respecting and acting upon what they receive in return. How else will we create a just and flourishing future.'

Linda Tucker, CEO Global White Lion Protection Trust and author of *Mystery of the White Lions*, *Saving the White Lions* and *LionHearted Leadership*

'This practical guide to communicating with animals contains a great deal of wisdom. I particularly enjoyed how the book placed animal communication in a broader spiritual context. For those with a truly open mind, this book is a treasure that can literally open up new worlds.'

Richard Thoburn, Founder, Burnie's Foundation,
www.burniesfoundation.com

'In Animal Communication Made Easy, *Pea gives a simple, clear and concise guide to communicating with our animal friends. For anyone interested in learning how to have a deeper relationship with their own pets and in communicating with other animals, this is the perfect handbook – practical, factual and easy to follow.'*

Dr Richard Allport MRCVS, VetMFHom, BVetMed

'Pea Horsley is the real deal. A book of this quality could allow individuals an opportunity to understand their animals with additional insight, enabling them to understand early pain onset, and allowing a more preventative, rather than reactive, approach to their health care.'

Julia Robertson, Founder, Galen Therapy
Centre and Galen Myotherapy®

'Pea provides an easy-to-follow manual that covers all aspects of communication, from the basics through to full proficiency, and along the way helps us to avoid all the pitfalls, the biggest being lack of self-belief. I so enjoyed this chance to take a refresher course from this master communicator.'

Tom Farrington MVB, MRCVS, VetMFHom

'I'm fascinated by just how much we don't know about the amazing animals we share our lives with. I've been involved with dogs for the last 30 years and have currently five rescues in my life. They are all wonderful. I'm not as receptive as they are, but I'm learning. It's why I'm going to study Pea Horsley's extraordinary work and try to understand her great skills of communication. Even if a bit rubs off it will have been worth it. I heartily recommend this book.'

Peter Egan, Animal Advocate and Actor

Animal Communication

Made Easy

Also in the *Made Easy* series

The Akashic Records

Astrology

Chakras

Connecting with the Angels

Connecting with the Fairies

Crystals

Discovering Your Past Lives

Energy Healing

Feng Shui

Goddess Wisdom

Lucid Dreaming

Mediumship

Meditation

Mindfulness

NLP

Numerology

Qabalah

Reiki

Self-Hypnosis

Shamanism

Tantra

Tarot

Animal Communication

Made Easy

Strengthen Your Bond and Deepen Your Connection with Animals

Pea Horsley

HAY HOUSE

HAY HOUSE INDIA

New Delhi • London • Sydney

Carlsbad, California • New York City

Published in India by:
Hay House Publishers India, Muskaan Complex, Plot No.3,
B-2 Vasant Kunj, New Delhi 110 070
Tel: (+91) 11 4176 1620
www.hayhouse.co.in

Published in the United Kingdom by:
Hay House UK Ltd, The Sixth Floor, Watson House
54 Baker Street, London W1U 7BU
Phone: +44 (0)20 3927 7290
www.hayhouse.co.uk

Published in the United States of America by:
Hay House LLC, PO Box 5100, Carlsbad, CA 92018-5100
Tel: (1) 760 431 7695 or (800) 654 5126
www.hayhouse.com® • www.hayfoundation.org

Published in Australia by:
Hay House Australia Publishing Pty Ltd, 18/36 Ralph St,
Alexandria NSW 2015
Tel: (61) 2 9669 4299
www.hayhouse.com.au

Interior images: Shutterstock

First Hay House India Edition 2024

ISBN: 978-81-19554-85-0

Printed at Repro India Limited

For Texas,
friend, co-author and dog-training master.

You came into my life as a six-month-
old kitten and have been a powerful
healing force ever since.

You are my world.

I love you!

Contents

List of Exercises

List of meditations

Introduction

I had no idea animal communication even existed.

Back in 2004 I was working in theatre stage management in London's West End and touring all over the UK and internationally. Then I adopted my first dog and life was never the same again. In came Morgan, a delightful Beagle cross, and with him a whole new direction in life. He was my 'dogalyst'. He introduced me to animal communication and now it's my turn to introduce it to you. You can call me your 'humanalyst'!

Before we explore animal communication, let me explain a little of my journey and then I hope my path to animal communication will inspire you to start walking down your own path to communicating with animals, and then keep walking.

I would not say I have a gift. I knew nothing about animal communication when I started out and was pretty sceptical. I was a person who liked convincing evidence. The evidence came when I attended my first animal communication workshop.

When Morgan arrived from the Mayhew animal rescue, he lay in his bed and I felt deep sadness coming from him. Having grown up with cats, I didn't really know dogs, and I thought I must be doing something wrong. Then the rescue contacted their mailing list about an animal communication workshop and I thought, *Great, I'll get to understand what I'm doing wrong with Morgan*. At that time I believed, mistakenly, that animal communication simply involved reading an animal's body language.

So I went to the workshop and there were 20 of us in a circle listening to stories of a Doctor Doolittle nature. The teacher was explaining how it was possible to talk to horses and hear them talk back. Nineteen people were on the edge of their seat, crying as they listened, then there was me, arms crossed, legs crossed, and no doubt a frown on my face. I thought it was a load of codswallop. I didn't believe a word of it. It was so far out of my life experience, let alone comfort zone, that I nearly walked out at lunchtime, but something made me stay.

I am so glad I did, because then something incredible happened. We were partnered up in the afternoon and asked to communicate with each other's animal, and

I witnessed students receiving information that they couldn't possibly know. One, because the animal and their human guardian were complete strangers to them, and two, because they were working from a printed photograph of the animal and were therefore unable to reach conclusions based on body language. I know – bizarre, right? How is that even possible? Well, more on that later.

We were told to hold our partner's animal photograph face down and feel what the species was. I thought, *How the heck am I supposed to do that?* And that it was a bit pointless really, because we were in central London and for that reason it was most likely to be a dog, cat or rabbit.

I held the photo face down between my hands and silently addressed my question to it: 'What species are you?' And I heard a word in my mind: 'Rabbit.' Turning the photograph over, I discovered that I was right. *Lucky guess*, I thought, and dismissed it.

Then we were told to ask the animal some questions and to write down whatever came to us. The first question was: 'What's your favourite food?'

I repeated the question silently in my mind and saw one of those dream-like images in my mind's eye. It was green leaves. But the rabbit's guardian explained that wasn't his favourite food.

It would have been very easy at that stage to declare 'Well, this isn't working' or 'I can't do it.' But when we start anything new it often begins that way. Mo Farah wasn't instantly a gold medal winner and Usain Bolt didn't start out as the fastest man on Earth. They practised. A hell of a lot.

The second question was: 'Who's your best friend?'

Again I saw an image, this time of an espresso coffee-coloured rabbit. It turned out that the rabbit did have a rabbit friend that colour and that they were a bonded pair. *Another lucky guess*, I thought.

Then the third question was asked: 'What's your favourite activity?'

I got a sense of a sofa, but quickly dismissed it. Little did I know this was a house rabbit. And why the sofa? Because his favourite activity was watching TV. It's true. He liked to sit on the sofa every Saturday evening and watch *You've Been Framed*. I'm not kidding.

To be honest, that experience did not convince me that I really was communicating with an animal. What got my attention was when my designated partner, a complete stranger who was holding a photo of my ginger cat, Texas, described my hallway, which is very distinctive, where my sofa was positioned and its colour, and Texas's favourite thing to sit on in the garden and where it was located. It was just as if he'd given her a private tour of our home behind my back. It had me baffled. I wanted to know how that was possible.

That day was a turning point in my life. In hindsight, it appears I had a cat-alyst too. If Texas had decided not to communicate that day, things would have turned out very differently.

As an animal lover, I wanted to know more. If this was really happening, it would have much larger implications. I could talk to animals I knew, I could talk to wildlife in my garden and maybe I could talk to species like lions, dolphins and whales. I wondered what it would be like to communicate with these different species and what they might want to express. Questions started springing up from left, right and centre. I was excited by the thought of knowing what their feelings were, what they loved and what they feared, and what they thought about their life and human beings. Would they have advice for us? Could they tell us how to help the planet?

I attended another workshop out of a desire to know more, and that was when I had my lightbulb moment: I realized I wanted to be a professional animal communicator. I'd already decided to leave the theatre and return to my first love, animals, I just didn't know what form that would take. I'd gone through dozens of animal-related jobs and knew it was none of them. It was only when Morgan appeared and brought me to animal communication that the realization dawned that this was it. Animal communication was the occupation that I was being drawn to; I just hadn't known what it was called, or that it existed.

Over the next 12 months I did everything necessary to make that dream come true. I really wanted to express my passion for animals and to make a positive difference to their lives and wellbeing. I'd had 15 years of a very successful career working with people like Harold Pinter, Edward Fox, Richard Wilson and Warren Mitchell, but now I'd found something I wanted to do even more – something that really ignited my light.

Months later, I was in my back garden sitting at a table with a silver parasol and practising animal communication with a case study. When I'd finished, I sat back in my chair, enjoying the sun's rays and inner city silence. Something caught my attention and I glanced over to my left hand. A metallic green fly with black bristly back legs had landed on it.

I thought to myself, I wonder if this fly can hear me?

'Hello,' I said out loud to him.

I thought he'd fly off, but he remained there and it felt as though he was waiting. This was my first attempt at communication with any kind of insect, let alone a fly, and I wondered how I could be sure we were really connected.

I said to him, 'If you can hear me, please fly around this parasol and come back and land on my hand.'

Without a moment's hesitation, the fly took off from my hand, flew anti-clockwise around the parasol and came back to land on my left hand.

'That's pretty impressive,' I said. I looked into his maroon-coloured eyes and asked, 'Can you do it again?'

The fly took off, sunlight gleaming through his translucent wings. Again he flew anti-clockwise around the parasol and came to rest on my left hand. Both times anti-clockwise, both times my left hand. Was this a coincidence or was this evidence the fly could hear me and was choosing to act on my request?

I said, 'Please fly around this parasol one more time for me. If you do, I promise you I will never question whether animal communication is possible again.'

The moment I'd finished asking, he was in the air and flying around the parasol, again anti-clockwise, then coming back to land on my left hand.

He looked up at me expectantly, as if he was waiting for my reaction.

'Incredible! Thank you!' I said, astonished. I was feeling so many emotions – excitement, amazement and respect.

As soon as I'd thanked the fly, he flew away, as if his mission with me had been completed. I remained sitting, taking in everything that had just happened. It felt such a blessing to be shown so clearly that even tiny species are capable of inter-species communication.

More significantly for me, the fly ambassador had managed to silence my sceptical mind. From that moment on, I started to approach other species with a new-found appreciation. Now if a fly comes into my house, rather than thinking of ways to eliminate it, I open a door or window and ask it to leave. Sometimes I'll add, 'This is the way out.' I've found this method works nearly every time. Often the fly has just come inside by accident and can't wait to be out again.

In 2006 I took a leap of faith and left my theatre career to start over. I've been working full time with animals ever since. I've taught workshops to people aged from eight to 89 and toured worldwide. I hold regular communication-based retreats with wild animals in their natural habitat and have taken small groups to Egypt, Panama and Hawaii to communicate with dolphins, turtles, whales and manta rays. As well as teaching people how to communicate with their own animals, I also offer consultations, and have communicated with thousands of animals all over the world.

This has felt like a calling to me. I feel it's an honour to be an ambassador for animal communication, sharing a method that is so simple in itself yet reaps such profound and healing results for human and non-human animals alike. I honestly believe animal communication is our natural super power, an ability we are all born with and a tool we can all use, and it's the most powerful and immediate way we have to re-establish a loving and meaningful relationship with the natural world.

I'm certain I don't have all the answers yet, but in this book I will share with you the most useful elements of what I've learned from my own trials and errors, struggles and successes.

There is a tremendous power in being able to communicate with animals. It can help you, your animals and any other species you encounter. You have the chance to make a difference, both personally and through the ripple effect of your daily choices, which can bring healing, health and harmony to other species.

You might think you're only going to learn how to chat to your animal companions, and possibly wild animals and those of the sea and the air, but in reality you're going to learn *so much more*. Principally, you'll learn to listen with your heart.

In essence, animal communication teaches you to become more aware, more connected and more respectful. As you gain a greater awareness of the interconnected web of life, it inspires you to protect and nourish the natural world.

By learning animal communication I can pretty much guarantee you'll soon be experiencing incredible connections with animals. As you'll learn over time, it's very practical, healing, loving, mind-expanding *and* incredibly deep.

Pay attention, dear friends. This book will change your life.

Part I

THE WORLD OF ANIMAL COMMUNICATION

'Somewhere, something incredible is waiting to be known.'

CARL SAGAN, ASTRONOMER

Chapter 1

Overview of Animal Communication

'The beginning is the most important part of the work.'

PLATO, PHILOSOPHER

Let's start at the very beginning. Before we modern humans tippy-tapped at our computer keyboards and chattered away to teeny-tiny people crammed inside a tiny oblong box called a mobile or cell phone, we were in tune with our natural environment. Then we developed language, advanced technologically and declared ourselves 'intellectually superior', and in doing so we lost touch with what really mattered: nature. But it wasn't always that way.

Indigenous cultures still recognize the spirit in all living things, including animals, trees, plants, the ocean and rocks. These cultures often have a way of understanding and communicating with animals, nature and the environment that is very different from the approach of mainstream society.

In Australia, an Aboriginal man explained, 'Aboriginals see themselves as part of nature. All things on Earth we see as part human.'[1]

Native Americans call all living beings 'our relations'. They honour the spirit of every furry, finned and feathered creature, and the scaly and crawly ones too. They believe that everything on Mother Earth is related, dancing together in the cycle of life.

So animal communication is nothing new. It's just something we modern humans have neglected because we've come to rely mainly on verbal language as a form of communication. Our ancestors were communicating with animals, and we can too. But the truth is many of us modern *Homo sapiens* are suffering 'separation sickness'. We crave connection more than anything, because our instinctual desire is to be in connection with nature, recognizing on a soul level that we are part of it. Yet as we're progressing with technology, we're moving further and further away from nature connection and meaningful relationships.

The good news is that many people do have intuitive communication with animals, and in some cultures it is still an active practice. It's also true we understand quite a lot without intuitive communication. We get it when our cat sits between us and our laptop, or lies across our arms. Some cats will even sprawl across the keyboard, which isn't subtle at all. We get it when our dog pushes a toy into our legs or gives a series of high-pitched barks by the door when they see a squirrel outside. We understand when our horse gives us a gentle nuzzle or kicks over their empty feed bucket.

Animals give us physical and audible cues because they've learned we don't always notice the subtle ones. Instead, we ignore them or mistake what they're communicating to us.

In return, we feel we have to be really obvious back and believe a cuddle, a shout or a shove are the only forms of communication our animals understand. In human culture we view communication as language. Oh, how limited we've become!

It's time to wake up now. Times are changing. The barriers are breaking down and people are remembering their real connection to animals and nature.

The ethics of speciesism

Let's look at the value that's often assigned to animals on the basis of their species membership.

The term 'speciesism' was coined by British psychologist Richard D. Dyer in 1970 and then popularized by the Australian philosopher Peter Singer. It's the idea that being a human animal is a good enough reason to have greater moral rights than all non-human animals.

Pure speciesism carries the idea of human superiority to the extreme of saying that the most trivial human wish is more important than the vital needs of other species. For example, a speciesist would say it was acceptable for animals to be treated cruelly and killed in order to provide fur for humans to wear as decorative coats and collars, scarves, bobbles on hats or fobs on keyrings.

People who justify this belief declare that human beings are more self-aware and more able to choose their own course of action than other animals. This, they say, enables them to think and act morally, and so entitles them to a higher moral status.

This view is often condemned as the same sort of bigotry as racism or sexism. Not only this, but scientific evidence says otherwise.

The Cambridge Declaration on Consciousness

> *'I think; therefore I am.'*
>
> René Descartes, philosopher

On 7 July 2012 at the Francis Crick Memorial Conference on Consciousness in Human and Non-Human Animals, an international group of prominent cognitive neuroscientists, neuropharmacologists, neurophysiologists, neuroanatomists and computational neuroscientists gathered to discuss whether animals were conscious.

Crick, the co-discoverer of DNA, had spent the last years of his career studying consciousness and in 1994 he had published a book about it called *The Astonishing Hypothesis: The scientific search for the soul*. The outcome of his memorial conference was the Cambridge Declaration on Consciousness, which concluded: 'Non-human animals have the neuroanatomical, neurochemical, and neurophysiological substrates of conscious states along with the capacity to exhibit intentional behaviors. Consequently, the weight of evidence indicates that humans are not unique in possessing the neurological substrates that generate consciousness. Non-human animals, including all mammals and birds, and many other creatures, including octopuses, also possess these neurological substrates.'[2]

So, top scientists have proven and are publically proclaiming what many of us animal lovers have always known: animals are conscious. They are aware beings, with intelligence and the ability to recognize themselves, experience emotions and make decisions. Therefore, they can no longer be viewed as inanimate objects without feelings.

For too long we've denied animals' pain and suffering and considered our actions towards them as acceptable because 'animals don't feel'. Nothing could be further from the truth, and what may be even more shocking is that the animals are aware of what we are doing to them.

Imagine for a moment being an animal who is treated as an object or product and is discarded for 'breaking down' or not being 'fit for purpose'. How would that make you feel? It isn't comfortable when you see it from their point of view, is it? Yet many animals are treated this way.

The scientists who signed the declaration agree that the cheerful dog on your sofa or the resplendent cat on your lap and all of the other creatures in your life are not insensate machines – they are glorious, bright and sentient beings who experience consciousness. Non-human animals are just like us. Or to put it another way, we are just like them!

Recognizing and acknowledging our similarities makes communicating with non-human animals so much easier.

Animal communication in a teeny-weeny nutshell

Animal communication is an exchange of energy over a distance between a human and non-human animal or between two non-human animals. It can also be referred to as 'interspecies communication' or 'intuitive animal communication'. It's an intuitive exchange of non-verbal information and a universal language across species.

The key to it is that it functions on the frequency of love, otherwise known as 'heart consciousness'.

It's quite easy to mistake an animal communicator for a 'horse whisperer' or 'dog listener', who reads an animal's body language and understands the psychology of a particular species. But communication with animals is very different from the work of an equine, canine or feline behaviourist. Neither is it about 'reading' an animal. Animal communication is a two-way exchange of information that is more akin to a silent conversation.

In animal communication information is sent and received non-verbally between two animals – one human and one non-human – through the use of the senses. We're going to look at this in depth in the next chapter and explore how it relates to you, but to begin with, it's important to know that you were born with the ability to communicate with other species of the animal kingdom of which you are a part. This is a completely natural skill that we're all born with. We all originated from the same 'root', but somehow we've forgotten that *we are animals too.*

Re-membering

Children remain in tune with their intuition and maintain their unquestionable connection with animals. As children, we can chat away quite happily to our cat or dog friends, the birds and any other species we encounter. It's only when we develop into teenagers and then adults that we start to be influenced by our parents, teachers, peers and colleagues and ignore our gut instincts and our innate knowing.

So it's very common for the ability to communicate with animals to be lost after childhood, but where a love for animals remains and there is a willingness to relearn, the skill can be recovered or, as I often describe it, 're-membered', which refers to when we 'member' ourselves back into the animal kingdom as an equal part of it.

Has your intuition crawled into a cave? Even if it has, it's always possible to coax it out into the light where it can be acknowledged, trusted and admired for being a valued aspect of who you are. Perhaps you're aware that you're feeling things that you can't readily explain. Have you ever gone house viewing and stepped through the door of a property and felt you didn't like the vibe of the place? If so, you've been perceiving intuitively. Or perhaps you've been thinking of a friend and then the phone rings and it's them – you've been subconsciously perceiving them.

You may already be aware of having intuitive feelings about your own animals or the animals you encounter. Maybe you've looked into the eyes of your animal and had the sinking feeling that something wasn't right and then your vet has confirmed it.

To some degree, all of us are intuitive. Quite how much depends how much we use our intuition and trust it. The more we use it, the stronger it becomes, like a muscle.

Where does animal telepathy come into it?

'Telepathic animal communication' refers to the same concept as 'animal communication'. They're simply different titles for the same modality. I tend to drop the 'telepathic' tag because it's such a mouthful. You try saying 'telepathic animal communication' over and over again. It gets tiring. I also drop it because many people have the belief that they're not telepathic. Don't be intimidated by the term 'telepathy'. Truthfully, we're all telepathic because it's the same as being intuitive. Telepathy is finely tuned intuitive ability.

The word 'telepathy' comes from the Greek *tele*, meaning 'distant', and *pathy*, meaning 'feeling' or 'perception'. Telepathy can be seen as the silent transmission of a mental word or image. When you're communicating with animals, you're feeling information (receiving these transmissions) across a distance without any physical interaction.

I believe animal communication is very accessible, and if simplifying the terminology allows more people in, I'm all for that.

What does animal communication look like?

When you're watching someone communicating with an animal, there is very little to see. Most of the time they will have their eyes closed and be completely still as they concentrate on the link between themselves and the animal they're conversing with. The animal, on the other hand, who will be naturally skilled and have less need to concentrate on communicating, might be looking away, having a scratch or mooching off down a field. You see, animals already know they can communicate with us. We're the ones who need to remember we can communicate with them.

We are easily distracted and often find it hard to maintain concentration, which is why we prefer another human to face us so we can believe, at least, that they're listening to what we're saying and paying attention to it. But animals don't need to be looking into our eyes to 'hear' us. Cats who attend my workshops as guest teachers - that's what I call them and truly that's who all the animals are who come into the space - will often show themselves for a moment then go and sit behind something, out of view. I'm often told to share the message: 'I can hear you from over here.' In this way, with very little effort, they teach a basic principle: animal communication is flexible.

The benefits of animal communication

> *'Every animal knows more than you do.'*
>
> Chief Joseph, leader,
> Nez Perce Native American tribe

There is so much to be gained from reigniting our natural ability to communicate with animals. It can contribute to a deeper appreciation for other animals and a deeper understanding that we can be in kinship with all of life. There is also a larger view, where we gain a greater affinity for the environment and sustainability. Through the practice of animal communication, we start to remember our place as part of nature and develop a respect for the natural resources that support our life.

Imagine a world where ways of knowing, like animal communication, are recognized, valued and have an established place as legitimate forms of knowledge in academic and modern Western contexts. That is the world I envisage.

This book will recover and develop your skills in human-animal communication. You'll also find it helps you to deepen your human-nature connection.

Here are some real examples of how animal communication can be helpful.

Bailey's alarm call

Lynn told me that she and her teenage daughter, Sam, recognized animal communication was possible and very honestly admitted they had read lots of books on the subject but hadn't done very much else. Then one day their dog, Bailey, a Staffordshire bull terrier, was barking in Lynn's bedroom. This was very unusual, so Sam decided to stop the work she was doing in her own room to go and check it out.

When she walked into the room, Bailey sent her images of Ollie, one of their ferrets, running around it.

Sam searched the room, but Ollie wasn't there.

Sam reassured Bailey, who was very wary of the ferrets, that there were no ferrets loose in the room, then thought she'd better go and check the hutches in the back garden just in case they'd escaped.

Sure enough, Ollie, the ferret Bailey had shown to Sam, had somehow done a Houdini and escaped out of the hutch, and was now making his way towards the cat flap.

Although he couldn't see the hutch from the bedroom, obviously Bailey had an awareness of the ferrets' locations and *what they were doing, and his concern was quite well founded. He was worried that Ollie would come into the house, and that if he did, it wouldn't be long before he was in Lynn's bedroom, running all over the place. So, not only was he able to communicate his reason for barking, but Sam was able to receive it clearly and act on it.*

To summarize, a dog inside a house knew what a ferret who lived outside the house was doing, although he couldn't see him. Furthermore, the dog was able to communicate this effectively to his human, and the human received the message clearly and acted on it, proving that the dog was right all along. Good job, Bailey!

This story shows human-animal (dog) communication. It also demonstrates animal-animal (dog-ferret) communication. It gets you thinking, doesn't it? Lynn and Sam told me it encouraged them to study animal communication further.

This simple example shows the power of non-verbal communication between all species. When we remember we're animals too, it all makes perfect sense. It's inter-species communication, using a non-verbal universal language. How cool is that?!

The spider teacher

One of my animal communication students, Dawn Brumham, relates:

Last week I went into my bathroom and there was a huge spider in the bath. I always put them outside, but they always make me jump and the truth is I don't enjoy having to handle them. However, as per usual, I went to get a glass and small plate (to help coax the spider into the glass). But this spider just wouldn't go in. It kept jumping either side of the glass and I was getting frustrated. I was on my way out and didn't want to be late.

I remembered Pea's story about overcoming her fear of a snake, so I tried to send love to the spider and connect with it. I wasn't able to convince myself, though, and as a result neither was I able to convince the spider.

Then it hit me. I would ask my dog, who transitioned years ago, to help me. I asked him to speak to the spider and to tell it I wished it no harm.

Then I thought, Oh no, it will just hear the word 'harm', so I changed my thoughts and said to my dog, 'Tell it I just want to help it.'

Immediately there seemed to be a second of calmness and understanding from both parties. The spider then walked slowly, with ease, into my glass.

I then went to throw it out of the window of my bungalow, as I usually do, but just before I did, I had a very strong sense that this was not what was

> *wanted and that the spider wanted to be placed 'gently' out of the patio door onto some petals that were in a flowerbed.*
>
> *I obliged, because I felt a strong obligation to fulfil the request and honour the spider's trust in me. And all was well.*
>
> *The point I think I want to make is, once you have been on an animal communication course, it really does change everything.*

Now you've heard about a dog communicating with a human and a ferret, and a woman who communicated with her transitioned dog in order to communicate with a spider. Are you still with me?

I'm giving you these examples here because I want you to start seeing animals from a new perspective, and there's no better way than sharing a couple of true stories that I trust will grab your attention and pique your curiosity to know more.

Here's one more for you, which, if you share your life with a dog, might relate to an experience you've already had. By the way, there will be cats and other species in this book, too, and stories straight from the horse's mouth...

Whisper's fear

Whisper's guardian, Jean, wrote in and explained the problem she was having with her 17-month-old blue roan cocker spaniel:

He had several aggressive experiences between the ages of seven and nine months. I know this is the 'fear' period in a pup's development, but he changed from being a happy, loving soul into a very fearful little chap. He's now afraid of people he doesn't know and terrified of other dogs. I take him to training twice a week and have also had two separate dog experts helping me.

He's always been okay with my dogs, Shadow and Bluey, but outside his home environment he'll react aggressively if anyone tries to touch him or another dog comes up or invades his space. I've got to the stage where I'm struggling and becoming quite depressed because there seems to be little progress and he is going to have to spend the rest of his life on the lead and not have the joy of running free.

I have tried most things in the last 10 months, but however much I try to assure him he is loved, protected and safe, I don't seem to be able to predict or avoid his fearful explosions.

I have attempted to communicate with him myself, but I think I'm so emotional that I can't hear what he is saying.

I agreed to communicate with Whisper for Jean and then we talked through everything Whisper had discussed. After the consultation, Jean wrote to me again:

First of all, around the time you were communicating with him, he was very excited and happy. He also clearly communicated with me one day when we were on our own, much more clearly than at any other time; he sat looking at me and told me a nice lady was talking to him and he liked it.

The first week after your 'chat', there were two or three occasions when he reacted badly. I carried on communicating, as you suggested, with positive pictures and happy experiences.

The second week he was more relaxed and happy, and the wonderful thing for me was that we were communicating easily, which had been difficult with Whisper since his attacks.

Whisper eventually explained that he found it difficult to tell me how scared he was because he thought I'd be disappointed in him; he felt he should be able to protect me better. It broke my heart that this little soul had been struggling with this burden. I feel this exchange released a lot for both of us.

Last Thursday, Whisper and I had a trip on our own

> *to Bramham Horse Trials and I explained in advance what we were going to do. When he saw a group of dogs fairly close by, there was no fearful reaction and he even calmly watched horses warming up only metres away. It was the best day since the attacks and Whisper was very pleased with himself.*
>
> *Your communication and his consequent ability to talk to me have really given us a fresh start, and a new outlook on the whole problem. It has certainly given me new energy and a positive insight into what was, at times, a very depressing situation for the little chap and me. I know we're now on a very positive path.*
>
> *I'm sure there are many other people with fearful or reactive dogs who feel they can't quite understand the problem or see a way forward. Communication can really help.*

You're possibly asking yourself, 'How can I get to the point where I can resolve my dog's fear or reactiveness, or be informed that one of my animals has escaped? Wouldn't it be handy when negotiating with smaller species too?' This is what I'm going to teach you.

Let's start with a strong foundation

I believe in creating a strong foundation, like the roots of a tree, so that you can then grow and branch out in all directions. So I'd like to end this chapter with a meditation called 'The present moment', because being truly present with your animal is one of the most important starting points to communicating with them. It might seem simple, but even if you find it easy, I believe both you and your animal will enjoy this quiet, focused, together time.

Meditation and posture tips

Before I share the meditation, here are some guidelines that will be useful for all of the meditations included in this book:

- In some of the meditations you'll prefer to sit in a chair, while with others you might feel it's beneficial to lie down on the floor.
- If you're in a chair, choose a chair that will support your back but doesn't make you feel rigid and awkward.
- If you're lying down, completely surrender to the floor beneath you, relax all your muscles and let go. If you have backache, bend your knees and have your feet flat on the floor for extra support.
- When we meditate, our body temperature drops. To avoid feeling cold, wrap up nice and cosy in a blanket or shawl.
- You might also like to wear something baggy or

loose fitting to help you feel more comfortable.

- If you're sitting, try and sit with dignity, as this will help your focus. Avoid sitting either rigid or slumped.
- And above all else, take a moment to assess whether you've found the right time to engage with a meditation (or exercise). You don't want to have to rush it or worry about being interrupted. Timing is everything.

Meditation: The present moment

Think of an animal you love and move into the same space as them. If you have no animals in your life at the moment, you may like to try this meditation with a bird in your garden or a cow or sheep that you can see in a field. Observe for a moment what they're doing and whether they are busy or quite relaxed. It's okay to do this even if your animal friend is having a nap.

Once you're together, find somewhere comfortable you can sit and hold an image of the animal in your mind's eye, picturing them as clearly as you can. When you're ready, close your eyes.

Breathe in through your nose and then, as you breathe out through your mouth, relax and let go.

Breathe in again, hold for a moment, breathe out and relax. Allow your shoulders to gently fall away from your ears. Breathe in, pause, breathe out and deeply relax.

Continue to breathe in and out to your natural rhythm, and on every release of breath, allow yourself to sink deeper and deeper into relaxation.

Now bring your awareness to the image of your animal in your mind's eye. See them as clearly as you can and hold that image. Peacefully, gently, be together in this moment. It's your moment to be fully present, focused on your animal, on yourself and on this precious moment of togetherness.

If you feel your mind wandering, there is no need to stress, just refocus on the image of the animal and your togetherness. It's just you and them, present in this moment, together.

With gentleness and love, observe the image of your animal and your special connection. When was the last time you gave them this much time, this much focus? When were you last fully present with them? Undistracted? Unflustered?

Just relax now, focus and be aware of being in this present moment together. If you're connecting with an animal you don't know, like a bird, cow or sheep, notice what it feels like to share this moment with them, unhindered by an agenda or time constraints.

Your animal is a living, breathing, sentient being, just like you. They have a different exterior, a different coat, but at their core, they are just like you. They may have four legs, they may have wings, but they are just like you. The core is the same, no different.

Be with your animal and acknowledge their emotions, and how they express their feelings.

Be with your animal and acknowledge their opinions, and how they express what they like and dislike.

Be with your animal and acknowledge they have intelligence, and how they understand and process experiences.

Observe what it feels like to spend this time where you are still, calm, quiet and focused on being present with your animal.

You might notice that you find it hard to be calm and relaxed at the moment. Maybe you are struggling to keep your focus and are distracted by lots of different thoughts. If that's the case, this practice is even more vital for you. The calmer and quieter you are, the easier you'll find it to communicate.

Take one last moment to confirm what you're feeling, and quietly, in your mind, thank your animal for this experience.

Then open your eyes, trusting that, even if they haven't looked as though they were engaging with you, your animal has been very aware of your intention and desire to be connected and together.

Being present with an animal in togetherness can deepen our relationship and improve the lines of communication. When we truly acknowledge animals for being sentient, intelligent and conscious, it will in turn enhance our bond with them. It's a blessing that can transform our whole relationship.

You can repeat this meditation a few times a week until it feels like second nature. The length of time is not so important, but regular repetition is key. A few minutes of quiet and calm, just being present with an animal you love – what could be better? Bliss!

SUMMARY

- Animal communication is not new; our ancestors communicated with animals, and indigenous cultures still do.
- World-class scientists have proven that animals are conscious, have emotions and have mirror self-recognition.
- We're all born with the ability to communicate with animals, because it's based on intuition and the universal language of energy.
- There is much to be gained by re-membering this innate skill.

Chapter 2

Shifting Perspective

'Change the way you look at things and the things you look at will change.'

DR WAYNE W. DYER, PHILOSOPHER

Let's start out with some home truths:

- Everyone can communicate with animals.
- It's not a gift.
- Everyone is intuitive.
- Animal communication is easier with an open mind.
- Animals understand a lot more than we realize.
- We're the ones who have forgotten how to listen to them.
- The biggest barrier to communicating with animals is ourselves.

If we examine these in a little more detail, we can change our perspective and understand how to break down any barriers that may be preventing us from communicating with animals.

Communication

Learning language

It has been widely claimed that humans learn language using brain components that are specifically designed for this purpose and that this linguistic ability makes us stand apart from and, many claim, above other animals. However, a recent study in the *Proceedings of the National Academy of Sciences of the United States of America* reveals brand new scientific evidence that strongly suggests that language is learned in 'ancient general-purpose systems' that *pre-date human existence*.[1]

'This discovery contrasts with the long-standing theory that language depends on innately-specified language modules found only in humans,' says the study's senior investigator, Michael T. Ullman, PhD, professor of neuroscience at Georgetown University School of Medicine.

The study of 665 participants found that children learned their native language and adults learned second languages using ancient brain circuits that were also used for a wide variety of other tasks.

Here's the juicy detail: 'These brain systems are also found in animals,' said co-author Phillip Hamrick, PhD, of Kent State University.

Behind verbal communication

Breaking down verbal communication, we realize that there is much more going on than the words. We use words to describe things, which could be places, people, feelings or objects. Behind these words there is a telepathic world that helps us form an imagined experience. For example, if someone is telling you about their holiday, they might describe their fantastic hotel and the pristine beach. As they talk through their experience, you'll be forming images in your mind of what you think the hotel and beach look like, and emotionally you'll be imaging what the hotel and beach feel like. It's in our nature to try and understand something more fully, and we do this, sometimes quite subconsciously, by trying to recreate the experience someone is explaining.

And there are other forms of communication that go even further beyond the spoken word...

Beyond verbal communication: animal intuition

In 2006 I was invited round to the home of microbiologist Rupert Sheldrake, PhD, for lunch, because he wanted to discuss my experiences with animal communication. He had conducted a well-known study on whether animals were able to know when their people were coming home, using statistical analysis and controlled experiments with a number of different animals, and had written a book about it called *Dogs That Know When Their Owners Are Coming Home*.[2] If you're evidence minded, you'll find it an interesting read.

The most extensive records concerned a mongrel terrier called Jaytee and his guardian, Pamela Smart. Pam had adopted Jaytee from Manchester Dogs' Home in 1989, when he was still a puppy. Then in 1993 she was made redundant and became unemployed. With no pattern to her life, she was away at random times and for different periods. Often her parents wouldn't know when she'd return, but Jaytee always seemed to anticipate her homecoming.

Sheldrake conducted a two-stage investigation:

1. In stage one, Pam and her parents kept a log of when she went out and Jaytee's reactions. Pam kept another record of where she went, her method of travel, how far she'd travelled and the time she set off to return home. Out of 100 occasions observed, Jaytee reacted 85 times by waiting for Pam by the front window approx. 10 minutes before she'd return. That's 85 per cent accuracy! The data showed that Jaytee was reacting to the moment Pam decided to return home, and it didn't matter how long she'd been out or how far she'd travelled.

2. In stage two, the Science Unit of Austrian State Television filmed Pam's parents' home continually and another film unit followed Pam when she went out. After three hours, 50 minutes, the film crew told Pam to go home. She took five minutes to walk to a taxi rank and arrived home 10 minutes after that. When they played the footage on TV, they did a split-screen so both Pam's home, with her parents and Jaytee, and Pam out and about could be observed at the same time. While Pam was out, Jaytee lay relaxed at her mother's feet. When Pam was told to return home, Jaytee's ears pricked and his attentiveness elevated. Exactly 11 seconds after Pam was told to go home, Jaytee crossed to the front window and sat there waiting. He stayed there until Pam arrived home.

There were no sensory clues in the form of cues from Pam's parents (who had no idea when Pam would return), there was no familiar car noise or bus pulling up. There was nothing that could indicate Pam was coming home except Jaytee's own extrasensory perception. Once Pam had the intention to return, Jaytee knew.

Sheldrake reasoned that the method was telepathic communication. He concluded that animals 'have much to teach us about social bonds and animal perceptiveness, and much to teach us about ourselves'. I wholeheartedly agree. He went on to explain that the evidence he discussed in his book suggested 'that our own intentions, desires and fears are not just confined in our heads, or communicated through words and behaviour – we can influence animals and affect other people at a distance. We remain interconnected with animals and people we are "close" to, even when we are far away.'

Perspective

How do you view animals?

Take a moment now to ponder how you view animals. Make a few notes if you like. What is your current awareness of them? When you're ready, read on.

Did you include the following?

1. *Animals think, feel and reason.* They can make decisions, have personal preferences and act on their decisions, or not, as they choose. They're not dumb. They have free will. Just like us.

2. *Animals are emotionally complex.* They fall in love, they have best friends, they dislike some individuals and they have cross-species relationships. You only have to surf the internet and you'll discover hundreds of examples of different species caring for each other, like the elephant and dog who were best friends and adored one another, or the hippo and the Jack Russell. There's also the giant Aldabra tortoise who'd cared for a baby hippo who had been made

an orphan by the 2004 tsunami. Humans care for their own species and other species too. It's another animal and human similarity.

3. *Animals have all of the emotions we label human.* They have the ability to feel happiness, love, frustration, anger, rage, insecurity, wariness and confusion, and all the other emotions too. The wonderful thing about a lot of species is their capacity for forgiveness. This is one of the many lessons animals teach humans. We excel at guilt. We can get locked in it. Animals do not feel guilt as strongly as we do. Perhaps they know it has no benefit long term. It would be interesting to ponder on that for a while. Why do we excel at guilt? Is it part of our conditioning? Wouldn't it be more helpful to excel at forgiveness instead?

How do you view yourself?

You may be viewing animals differently by now, but the biggest shift of consciousness involved in animal communication is in how we view *ourselves*: the human animal.

We are capable of perception beyond our five senses. We have our sixth sense – our intuition, our gut knowing. You can call it an extra-sensory perception. What's great is that it's something we're born with. To expand, refine and harness it, we need to acknowledge it. And there's a lot of fun to be had in doing that. More on this later. In the meantime, let's face reality.

The 'real reality'

> *'Every one of us is, in the cosmic perspective, precious.'*
>
> CARL SAGAN, ASTRONOMER

There is no difference between us and other animals. We're all animals of the animal kingdom. Yes, we look different, we eat differently and we have different skills. Just look at ants and their teamwork or dogs' ability to smell dis-ease or drugs. We humans have particular skills too, but when you break it all down, our core is the same. All animals breathe and have a heart. This is what I refer to as 'the core'. And when we reach out to another animal species, this is where we start.

So it really doesn't matter whether you're a dog, bear, cat, dolphin, horse, fly, lion, crow, snake, child, adult or butterfly, you share a primary similarity with other animals. Which means you can find ways of communicating with them. What might be standing in your way?

Barriers to communication

> *'At times you have to leave the city of your comfort and go into the wilderness of your intuition... What you'll discover is yourself.'*
>
> ALAN ALDA, ACTOR

I made a pretty bold statement earlier where I declared that everyone can communicate with animals. It's true, but there are also things that can hold people back. So let's begin to look into the principal barriers to animal communication.

1. We're trained to toe the line and follow a belief system that's not our own

It's very easy to adopt the views of others. When we're children, we're influenced by our parents and teachers and often accept what they say as 'read'. Before the age of five, we're in 'bath sponge mode', absorbing everything. Scientists call this 'the age of theta brainwaves'; our state at this time is similar to being in hypnosis, i.e. suggestible, or REM dream sleep. As we age, we're influenced by our peers and partners, then work colleagues and leaders. I come across a number of people each year who say something in a workshop, and in time they have the epiphany that it's their husband's voice speaking, or that of a work colleague, sometimes even a best friend, but not their own.

If we're open enough to say we're attending an animal communication workshop, the reaction of those around us can be incredulity or undermining laughter. 'You're doing what?!' 'Am I going to have to start calling you "Doctor Doolittle" now?'

All of this only undermines our desire to do, or even think, something new.

But we learn a lot of lessons in life that simply aren't true. Some of the most intelligent people on the planet don't accept that animal communication is real. They may be intelligent, but that doesn't make them right.

More to the point here, a limiting thought like *Animals can't communicate* is what actually prevents communication. So, if you're having any doubts about whether animal communication is feasible or whether you can do it, take a moment to seek out the source of those thoughts. Ask, 'Do *I* really believe that? What is *my* truth? Am I open to experiencing it for *myself*?'

Very quickly we can grasp if we've been holding on to thoughts and beliefs that are not our own. If you find that's been happening to you, write them down, rip them up, move on.

2. We shut our intuition out

Sometimes we shut out our own intuition, which in turn blocks us from communicating with animals. Why might this happen? Perhaps it comes from a concern about what we might receive. There could be a worry that the information will be too painful and so a barrier is put in place to prevent it from reaching us.

3. Our ego shouts!

The human self or ego's capacities for self-awareness, self-reflection and self-control are essential for reaching our goals. Nevertheless, the ego self has a perpetual desire to be seen in a positive light. So, as Mark Leary, professor of psychology and neuroscience at Duke University in North Carolina, USA, explains, 'While the self can be our greatest resource, it can also be our darkest enemy.'[3] As another researcher put it, the self engenders 'a self-zoo of self-defense mechanisms'.[4]

Let's talk more about this pesky ego and how it affects our animal communication.

The voice of the ego

Fear and desire

The ego voice can be one of fear and also one of desire.

The fear voice may sound a bit like this: 'I don't know if I can do this? What if I can't do this? What if everyone else can communicate with animals but me? What if I'm terrible?' If you happen to be sitting in a workshop, the ego fear voice might chime in with: 'What if I say what I've received from an animal and everyone laughs and I feel like a fool? I'm going to try and make myself invisible.' That's the self-defence mechanism in action.

The desire voice may sound a bit like this: 'I really, really, really want to do this. I want this so badly, I've not wanted anything so much in my whole life! I want to be outstanding at this because I love animals so much and want to help them.'

Good intentions are great, but if there's too much desire, it's as blocking to authentic communication as fear.

The importance of quietening the ego

After over a decade of communicating with animals, I've learned that the ego voice never goes silent. It's not meant to. I've also learned that it helps me recognize when I'm too focused on how I may come across, how well I may do or how much I am trying to control things. So it can be useful.

What's key is the volume of the ego voice. How loud is it? Does it drown out any messages that animals are trying to share with you?

The latest science of wellbeing shows that *transcending*, not enhancing, the self or ego is the most powerful and direct pathway to contentment and attaining inner peace.

In their book *Transcending Self-Interest: Psychological explorations of the quiet ego*, Heidi A. Wayment, PhD, and Jack J. Bauer, PhD, examine what social scientists have been observing for decades: that Americans are 'becoming more selfish, headstrong, and callous [and there is] a cultural slide toward narcissism.'[5] Without question, it's not only Americans.

The book's theories and research suggest two paths to transcending the ego, which may be summarized as:

1. Focus on creating a balance between your own self and others.
2. Cultivate self-awareness that isn't defensive, increase compassion and develop an interdependent self-identity.

At the end of these uniting paths lies a *quiet ego* - an ego less concerned with self-promotion than with the flourishing of both the self and others.

Turning down the volume of the ego

Here are two ways to reduce the volume of your ego:

1. Gratitude

My method to turn the volume of the ego voice down is to thank it. Yes, literally, offer it gratitude. Because it has shown me something.

When I'm thanking my ego, I might say:

- 'Thank you for reminding me I am not open enough, or neutral enough, or focused enough, on being present with this animal.'
- 'Thank you for showing me that my focus is on myself, my ego, rather than on holding the space for this animal to express themselves to me.'
- 'Thank you for showing me that I need to continue to work on turning down the dial on my ego voice.'

2. Selflessness

Another way of transcending the ego so it grows quieter is to embody selflessness. This way we can encourage the ego to be wiser, kinder and more compassionate towards others.

The voice of the higher self

There is another voice you might hear as you think about trying animal communication – that of your higher self, your cheerleader if you like. This will be totally different from the voice of the ego. Your higher self will sound more like this: 'Just calm down, you'll be fine. You're going to be okay. I believe in you. Give it a try and relax, you've got nothing to lose.'

This voice is only ever encouraging, positive and compassionate. It supports you and understands you. It is like a friend who holds your hand every step of the way.

Listen to this one.

The quantum solution

> *'It's all about love.'*
>
> TEXAS, CO-AUTHOR AND FELINE IN RESIDENCE

Texas turned up as I started this section and said I didn't need to write anything other than: 'It's all about love.' So, as I like to honour animals' wishes and I learned a long time ago to trust their teachings, there you are.

He's right, of course. Love is what binds us to animals and makes communication with them possible. But perhaps you're interested in a little scientific summary first? If not, skip this bit and get on to the juicy stuff further on.

Science sees sense ... happy dance!

> *'Reality is merely an illusion, albeit a very persistent one.'*
>
> ALBERT EINSTEIN, THEORETICAL PHYSICIST

Science used to declare that you and your dog (or cat or any animal you want to think about) were separate, that there was a division between you and them. That was Industrial Age thinking. Back in the day we were taught that we and our dog (again, substitute the species of your choice) were two totally separate beings in the same room and that concept seems to have become our Groundhog Day. Modern society seems stuck on this obsolete truth.

The new truth (or paradigm) is that you and your dog (again, substitute the species of your choice) are together. Not separate. Not divided. The development of science has led to the recognition of invisible connections between things that appear separate from each other in space or space-time. That's how Jaytee knew when Pam was returning home. Every one of us is part of this interconnected universe, not separate from it. I know, mind-blowing, eh?

In her book *The Field*, lecturer Lynne McTaggart reveals, 'The human mind and body are not separate from their environment but a pocket of pulsating power constantly interacting with this vast energy sea, and that consciousness may be central in shaping our world.'[6] According to philosopher Wayne Dyer, McTaggart has been able to present 'the hard evidence for what spiritual masters have been telling us for centuries'.

The truth is we're not stuck in the third-dimensional reality we think is 'it'. We're made of tiny pockets of quanta, pulsating points of power that dance together across any space and any time. Animals are made up of dancing quanta too.

'Come on in, the water's lovely'

To put it another way, we're all sub-atomic particles swimming together in the deep blue ocean of life called 'consciousness'. We're connected to an unlimited consciousness with no walls because we are also part of this consciousness. There are no barriers or boxes to consciousness and there are no barriers or boxes in animal communication.

Scared of water? See consciousness as a spider's web if you like. A web that you're on, I'm on, and the animals we love are on too. In fact, it's pretty crowded, because everything that exists and all their memories are there as well. And the threads of the web connect us to one another.

If this is bamboozling you, look at it from the point of view of one of my clients' cats: 'We're all soup in a bowl!'

In the quantum field, energy and matter are interchangeable. This has been researched and proven by top scientists. The concept feels so utterly mind-blowing and opens so many new possibilities that very few people have harnessed its power, or to put it more accurately, *our* power – the incredible power of our consciousness. It's time we changed that.

'Harness your power, Skywalker'

> *'Feel the force.'*
> YODA

It's time to shift from the materialist and mechanistic world and get up off the sofa to explore a worldview that is much, much more exciting. And real.

Forgive me for going all *Star Wars* on you, but there is a force. It's a force that connects us to one another, animals, our environment and the universe.

The force is so bright, soft and powerful that when you suspend your beliefs, become willing to set aside certainty and surrender to its illumine-sense, your life changes for the better. See how I split that word up? You will feel (sense) illuminated. You'll be more awake and aware of the world than most folks moving from A to B.

It makes sense to be illuminated

'Luminous beings are we, not this crude matter.'

Yoda

Rather than continuing to live our lives within a very narrow range of experience, let's make a stand and use the incredible power of our consciousness and tune in to dimensions of reality beyond our five human physical senses. The truth is we are all connected to everyone, every animal and everything in the universe. So we can all jump out of the box. In fact, what box? I didn't know there was a box!

Just remember, you are not powerless. You are power-*full*.

Exercise: Exploring the force

I want to guide you in sensing force energy in a super-simple exercise that you can repeat as many times as you like. This is your first Yoda class in the power of the force!

- Stand with your feet apart and take a few deep breaths. Relax and clear your mind.
- Rub your palms together quite vigorously to make them warmer and more sensitive.
- Hold your hands chest-width apart in front of you with the palms facing each other.
- Slowly start bouncing your hands in towards each other, without touching. You might find there is a natural stopping point.

- Then glide your hands slowly apart until they're either side of your body.
- Next, close your eyes.
- Slowly bounce your hands in towards each other again.
- Notice what you sense, however subtle, and try to put words to it.
- Then glide your hands out again, noticing what you feel and where you feel it. Observe how that is different from when you bounce your hands in.
- This time bounce your hands in towards each other and observe any colour behind your eyes, temperature change or emotions that you're sensing.
- Then continue to note other impressions as you glide your hands out.
- Once more, bounce your hands in and tune in to even the slightest sensation as you bring your hands closer together. Is there a point where they don't seem to want to go any further?
- Now glide your hands out, observing the subtlest of impressions.

What might you have sensed? Here are some suggestions:

- *Temperature* – warm or cool
- *A breeze*, either across your hands or as you move your hands
- *Tingling* in your palms
- *Colour/s* behind your closed eyes
- *Resistance*, either as you bring your palms together or glide them apart
- *A 'rubber band' sensation*, as if you can only glide out so far

- *A chewing gum sensation*, as if you're stretching gum as you glide out
- *Magnetism or a pull* stopping your palms from touching or forcing them apart as they want to pull back together
- *Cotton wool* between your palms
- *A ball* between your palms
- *Emotions* that change as you change direction with your palms
- *Release* as you move your palms out
- *Expansion or freedom* as you move your palms out
- *Less sensation* either when you glide your hands apart or bounce in

We all have different words for how we sense energy, because we're all unique. Some people are more aware of temperature than colour, and so on. What's important to note is that you are sensing energy – a force that you can't see when you look down into that space between your palms.

If you didn't feel or notice anything when you did this exercise, just do it again a little later or tomorrow. Relax, go with the flow and breathe. With practice, you'll become aware of very subtle sensations or impressions. Don't give up. You're not a quitter, right?

Practising this exercise can also help you start to notice other elements of energy you may not have been in tune with the first time you did it. Play with it, have fun, enter into the joy of discovery. You have started to sense and name energy, and that's exciting. From here on, you can only improve your sensitivity to the subtle world that is all around us, connecting us all.

In the next chapter, we're going to look at how your thoughts and emotions are like radio waves being broadcast into this giant field, or web, or soup(!) of infinite possibility. Not only that, we're going to put these theories into practice by having you experience them for yourself.

SUMMARY

- Humans and animals both have the brain systems that are used for learning language.
- They both have five senses and a sixth sense of intuition.
- Animals think, feel and reason. Like humans, they have free will.
- Animals are emotionally complex and experience all the emotions we label 'human'.
- The principal barriers to animal communication are beliefs, fear and ego.
- We're all gifted with an incredible power that can light up our life and our connections with animals. It's time to feel the force!

Chapter 3

How Does It Work?

'The only real valuable thing is intuition.'

Albert Einstein, theoretical physicist

Animal communication is based on intuition, which is a natural attribute of both animals and humans. Yet intuition is challenging to define, despite the huge role it plays in our everyday lives. Steve Jobs called it 'more powerful than intellect'. I love that.

The author of *The Art of Intuition*, Sophy Burnham, says, 'I define intuition as the subtle knowing without ever having any idea why you know it. It's different from thinking. It's different from logic or analysis. It's a knowing without knowing.'

It has been said that people who are very intuitive have had a role model or mentor who encouraged them. It certainly helps to have someone assisting you and valuing your intuitive information. That's my role with this book. I'm happy to hold your hand page by page.

Intuition and the US military

The importance of intuition is demonstrated by the fact that the US military is investigating it, because it has helped troops to make quick decisions during combat that have ended up saving lives. They've started a programme called Enhancing Intuitive Decision Making Through Implicit Learning (not a very catchy title) to investigate how intuition works and offer insight into the scientific basis of it.[2] That is important, as many of the general public actually confuse intuition with the supernatural. It's so not supernatural - unless you feel that having intuition is natural and rather super, and then it is.

The impetus for the programme came from field reports that detailed a 'sixth sense' that alerted soldiers to an impending attack or improvised explosive device (IED). These included the cases of a company of Canadian soldiers in Afghanistan, who, after a Taliban ambush in the summer of 2006, said in hindsight that their intuition had set off a warning, and of Staff Sgt Richburg, who, after sensing something odd about a man at an Iraqi internet café, managed to save 17 café patrons from the improvised bomb he had planted there.

'Flex your muscle, intuitive'

> *'I feel there are two people inside me - me and my intuition. If I go against her, she'll screw me every time, and if I follow her, we get along quite*

nicely.'

KIM BASINGER, ACTRESS

In some cases, people find their intuition opens up after a dramatic event like a car accident. In others, people have experienced childhood trauma that has caused them to rely on their own inner compass. I also believe that children who are shy and struggle to fit in with other children often turn to animals for their personal relationships and subsequently develop a sensitive connection that supports intuitive animal communication.

In general, intuition can be compared to a muscle that needs exercise. To communicate with animals, it's important to strengthen it. It takes time to develop, although less time for those who flex it regularly and listen to the subtle cues around them. If you resonate as someone who's very logical or analytical, or you're someone who's been dismissed or ridiculed for expressing intuitive insights, you may find that your journey into animal communication takes a little longer and requires more patience and perseverance. There's nothing wrong in that. You're still capable. Your intuitive muscle just needs more gym time. In this chapter, we'll look at practical ways to boost intuition, along with two personality types: sensors and intuitives.

Sensors and intuitives

Modern-day psychologists are guided by pioneer Carl Jung's description of our personality traits.[3] Jung had a 60-year psychology practice and over that time he began to see different qualities in people. According to Virko Kask, a personality-type consultant, 'These differences, in fact, have always existed; already the Vedic texts describe thousands of years ago the same qualities that Jung has spoken of.'[4] He breaks them down into two personality types:

- *Sensor:* Kask suggests that if a person has strong *sensorics*, their primary source of information is via their five senses of smell, sound, sight, taste and touch – the forms they directly experience. These are the channel through which a person also receives information about their own 'wrong me', which Kask calls the 'false ego'. This is directly related to power, position, territory and beauty. You'll recall this is the ego voice we wish to quieten down.
- *Intuitive:* If a person has a strong *intuition*, then they get information from the subconscious. The subconscious is like a huge memory bank and permanently stores everything we experience.

When a strongly sensoric person sees a cardboard box, for example, they immediately experience the form and use that information directly as it is. When a strongly intuitive person sees a cardboard box, they see the same thing, but automatically review what information is already in the subconscious 'store' for this item.

A sensor prefers real, reliable, solid information. An intuitive prefers speed and depth of insight. This manifests in a couple of ways, and this is where it gets interesting.

- Intuitives learn to trust pattern recognition to help them understand information quickly and see things that aren't 'there'.
- Sensors have the same ability, but they don't trust it, and so they don't hone it. Instead, they trust things that can be verified in the 'real world'.

These different personality types help explain why some people (intuitives) pick up animal communication fairly easily, while others (sensors) require more practice and persistence and can get frustrated by their lack of progress. Sensors tend to analyse, seek proof and need communication to be logical. Intuitive people don't care too much about facts. They're more interested in the connections between them, the meanings and the results. They're already comfortable seeing what 'isn't there'.

It helps to know which type you are so that you can understand how you approach animal communication. If you're unsure, here are a few more clues:

- *Sensors* value family, tradition, old friends, taking action. Why? These are all rooted in the known and knowable, and as a result can be trusted. Sensors 'hold the fort'.
- *Intuitives* place more value on the cerebral arena, including perspectives, concepts, possibilities and paradigms. Their conversation will generally revolve around these areas and they will have little interest in small talk. Intuitives are 'trailblazers'.

Personally, I'm a quiet person who likes to observe and think, and finds small talk exhausting (although I do love to have a giggle with chums over a pina colada). If I have to attend a social function, I'd much rather experience a deep and meaningful exchange one to one than revolve on a superficial level around the room. Therefore, I resonate as an intuitive.

This distinction helps you when you're communicating with an animal and receive an image of something you already know, like a blue ball, for example, but struggle to know if it's from the animal or yourself. You might presume that because it looks like something you recognize, you must be making it up. But what it shows is that your intuition is stronger than your sensoric senses. When you go through the process of verifying information the animal has shared, you may discover, for example, that the dog's favourite toy is a blue ball. It looks different from the one you're visualizing because the one you're visualizing is from your personal computer, as it were.

I find that when I'm tracking missing animals, I'll bring to mind the wooden fencing image that's already in my subconscious. I see fencing like that when I'm on walks with my dog. What's important is that the missing animal has seen, passed by or gone through some wooden fencing that's similar to this. It doesn't matter that it's not exactly the same wooden fencing.

Ten traits of intuitive people

However you see yourself, there are ways of strengthening your intuition and, in turn, enhancing your animal communication skills. Here are 10 traits of intuitive people that you might like to try out for yourself:

1. Listening to the inner voice

Intuitive people listen to the guidance of their intuitive insights and gut feelings. From this moment on, I encourage you to pay attention to every intuitive prod and poke, dream or inspiration that you experience, rather than noticing it but not acting on it or just ignoring it completely. Make a point of giving your intuition some 'training time' by paying it some attention.

2. Making time for solitude

Intuitive people are often introverted, but, according to Sophy Burnham, 'Whether you identify as an introvert or extrovert, taking time for solitude can help you reconnect with yourself and provide time for deep thought.'

3. Getting creative

It's good to know that getting creative can boost your intuition. Try some creative writing, poetry, storytelling, painting or drawing and get your creative juices flowing.

4. Observing

Start tapping into your intuition by noting in a journal when you notice coincidences, have intuitive insights that are spot on or make connections that surprise you. I'm an observer: I watch for signs and I pay attention to them. They guide me. Rather than thinking they're random coincidences, I look for connection and meaning and consider them breadcrumbs from the universe.

5. Listening to the body

Have you ever started to feel sick to your stomach when you've known something was wrong? Or felt 'butterflies' in your stomach when attempting something new? They're called *gut feelings* for a reason.

There's a network of neurons lining our gut that is so extensive some scientists have nicknamed it our 'second brain'. Michael D. Gershon, an expert in neurogastroenterology and author of *The Second*

Brain, says, 'The second brain contains some 100 million neurons, more than in either the spinal cord or the peripheral nervous system.'[5]

When sharing information, sometimes people state, 'I just felt it,' or 'I just knew,' and they'll place both hands on their stomach. I will also *feel* if information resonates for me in my gut. It's my intuitive gut knowing. You have it too. Trust it.

6. Connecting empathically

The brain is naturally empathetic. We have 'mirror neurons' that connect our brain like Wi-Fi with people we observe. 'When you see a spider crawling up someone's leg, you feel a creepy sensation,' says Dr Keysers at Netherlands University of Groningen. 'Similarly, when you observe someone reach out to a friend and they are pushed away, your brain registers the sensation of rejection.'[6]

It's also possible to share this depth of empathy with non-human animals: we can 'step into the paws' of an animal and mirror their feelings (just as I believe animals can be empathic towards humans). Many of you reading this book will do this subconsciously – you're naturally empathic and that's why you're drawn to animal communication.

To boost your level of empathy, notice when you have an empathic feeling towards another being.

7. Paying attention to dreams

When you pay attention to your dreams, you're able to tap into your mind's unconscious thinking processes or the intuitive part of your brain. I've also found that people communicate with their animals during their dreams. A missing animal will sometimes let them know where they're hiding. Sometimes an animal will transmit if there's a problem with their health. It's also quite common for people to experience being with their animals who have passed over.

After Morgan transitioned, we met again in my dreams and I was able to run my hands through his fur and look into his eyes as if he was right beside me. It was an incredible experience that I'll never forget, and I know I'm not the only one to have been lucky enough to have had this sense of tactile reconnection – clients and students have had it too.

8. Relishing down time

I suggest that you allocate regular time to switch off the TV and radio, put down the mobile and tablet, and disconnect from all technological activity. Are you feeling confused? Does the thought of being in silence and not checking your social media every hour trigger cold sweats? Few things stifle intuition as easily as constant busyness, multi-tasking, connectivity to digital devices, stress and burnout. There's a handy app called *Moment* that will track how long you're on your phone and how many times you check it.[7] It's important to introduce down time for yourself so that your mind and body can rest and your spirit can shine more brightly. Just unplug. Do it.

9. Releasing negative emotions

Your intuition will serve you better if you're able to accept and let go of negative emotions rather than suppressing or dwelling on them. Burnham says, 'When you are very depressed, you may find your intuition fails. When you're angry or in a heightened emotional state ... your intuition [can] fail you completely.' Thankfully, a study published in the *Psychological Science* journal showed that being in a positive mood boosted the ability to make intuitive judgements in a word game.[8] I've also experienced strong negative emotions clouding my animal communication but a good mood aiding it.

Here's a heads-up, though: being impulsive is different from being intuitive. The impulse to bop someone on the nose is not necessarily intuition!

10. Practising mindfulness

Meditation and other mindfulness practices can increase intuition and compassion. They give us the ability to listen to our inner selves. Mindfulness can be defined as 'paying attention to one's current experience in a non-judgemental way'. Everything begins within us. How well do we know ourselves? By being more in touch with ourselves, we will find our communication with animals flows more easily.

The modes of communication

Now you've learned that animal communication is based on intuition and discovered the gym exercises to strengthen that muscle, let's look at *how* you actually communicate with animals.

A two-way conversation

I can't stress this enough: when we communicate with animals, it's a two-way conversation. It's silent and non-verbal, but it is a conversation. It's not reading them. Animals are not passive bystanders. There is an exchange of information, a willingness to engage, because, like us, other animals have free will.

So, the most useful place to be in when communicating with animals is a position of neutrality. Focus on being open and accepting of whatever the animal chooses to share with you. There is no need to try and force or manipulate a communication – you'll simply fail. Don't forget this is another sentient being you are hoping to connect with. Come from a place of respect, reverence and complete openness to the communication you receive. The animal will respond positively to this kind of approach. Remember, you're going to be entering into a two-way conversation and that both parties – both *species* in this case – have free will and the ability to decide, feel and reason.

A neutral position tool

Here's something for the toolkit you're going to compile as you progress through this book and, to quote Buzz Lightyear, 'into infinity and beyond'!

An easy way to get into the neutral position is to repeat this phrase three times:

> *'I am neutral and open.'*

Basic modes and beyond

We have five basic modes of both sending and receiving information: seeing, hearing, feeling, smelling and tasting. Animals have these five basic senses too. Earlier in this chapter I described these as *sensoric* senses. There is also the sixth mode, which is intuition, our sixth sense. Intuitives are capable of both sensoric and intuitive communication.

We use any and all of these modes in animal communication. Communicating this way is subtler and softer than the spoken word to which we're so accustomed as humans. In fact, animal communication can be a bit like driving a car: you often use more than one skill at a time and none are mutually exclusive or superior to each other. It's quite normal to start out being better at receiving with one or two modes, but which mode is strongest will vary between people. When I started out, I primarily received words and then pictures started to filter in. The last mode I connected with was smell. As you become more skilled, you'll be able to move effortlessly between modes, and you'll be more engaged with what you receive than how you receive it.

Images, pictures and video

I've started with this one because I've discovered people tend to be able to trust it the most. The best way to explain it is to remember what it's like to see pictures when we're dreaming – some so vivid that we feel we're in the dream itself. In our dreams we can process colour, contrast, shape and movement, just as when we're awake. When we're communicating with an animal, we can do the same.

Receiving images from your animal: If you were to ask a dog, 'What's your favourite walk?', you might see an image of a line of trees next to a body of water. It can be as simple as that, or you may, from your subconscious databank, know that the trees are alder or willow and that the water looks like a canal or a river.

When you're receiving images from an animal, you perceive them with your mind's eye rather than your actual eyes. They can be snapshots of random information or they can have a sequence that links together. Some people receive footage as if they're watching video.

It may seem that images drop into your mind as your animal is communicating something to you. You might see an image of their water bowl as they explain they're thirsty, or the back seat of your car as they communicate they want to go out for a walk.

Sending images to your animal: You can communicate with your animal by using images too. If you want them to be calm and to lie in their bed, you might visualize them lying calmly in their bed. If you're trying to communicate to your cat that you'd prefer them to pee *in* the litter tray, you can visualize them stepping in, relieving themselves, then stepping out again. If you accompany this short string of images with an emotion of joy, they'll understand that if they do this, you'll feel happy. Sometimes it's necessary to repeat the images a few times before the animal understands the request. And don't forget they don't have to do as you've asked and they may have an illness or injury that makes your request difficult.

Person type: The type of person who has this as their strongest mode will be someone who considers themselves very visual or who has a good visual memory or who works regularly with images – perhaps a painter or graphic artist or a designer.

Thoughts

This is when you receive thoughts from an animal. You're probably receiving thoughts from your animal a lot of the time, but you may not be aware of them. To hone this skill, you need to practise being a very attentive listener.

This method requires a mountain of trust. It tends to be the hardest method of receiving, because people struggle to trust that the information is from the animal themselves and isn't their own mind making it up. I'm often asked how you know the difference. Practice is the answer. Once you begin to resonate with the energy of the words, and understand whether they're from you or the animal, it's even possible to differentiate volume, pitch, rhythm and tone. This is a fun way to communicate.

Receiving thoughts from your animal: If you were to ask my feline co-author, Texas, 'What's your favourite food?' you'd receive a reply directly in your mind and hear the words 'Fish! Fish!' Most of the time you'll hear these thought forms with your own inner voice – in other words, it will sound just like you, like when you read a book.

You can also ask your animals what they hear. This is useful if they've gone missing or if something is scaring them and you're unsure what it is. Some species have very keen hearing. Horses' hearing is similar in range and tone to that of humans, but they can hear low to very high-frequency sound, in the range of 14 Hz to 25,000 Hz (the human range is 20 Hz to 20,000 Hz). Horses can also move their ears 180 degrees using 10 different muscles (compared to three muscles for the human ear) and are able to single out a specific area to listen to, isolate it and run the other way. This means they can respond to a training instruction at a very low volume. *You don't need to shout.*

The tricky thing about this particular mode is learning when you're projecting your own judgements and agenda onto the animal's information and when you're being open and neutral and allowing their thoughts and feelings to reach you clearly. We'll look at that later in the book.

Sending thoughts to your animal: It's really crucial to get this one right. If you want your dog to get off your sofa, there's no point communicating to them, 'Don't get on the sofa.' They won't connect with the 'don't' and will receive 'Get on the sofa.' And the more strongly you send the message, '*Don't* get on the sofa,' the more they'll believe you're asking them to *get on the sofa*.

Try to lose 'don't', 'won't', 'can't' and 'shouldn't' from your vocabulary when communicating with animals. Ask for what you *do want* and the subconscious picture will match.

Person type: A person who receives information from an animal via this method will be someone who works with words a lot, like a teacher, writer, speaker or someone who has to write reports, give presentations or spend time listening to or creating words.

Emotions

You're quite possibly already receiving your animal's emotions. You might sense when your dog is feeling sad that you're going out and they're being left behind. You might feel your horse's excitement when you're letting them out into the field, or your cat's fear when you're taking them to be checked at the vet's. I want you to notice *where* you feel the emotions.

Receiving emotion from your animal: Just think how helpful it would be to be able to ask your cat how they feel about the new cat sitter. You might receive a feeling of joy, indignation, uncomfortableness or wariness. The same question can be asked of your dog: 'What do you feel about your overnight boarding experience?' If the response is received as a feeling of anxiety and nervousness, perhaps even fear, you know that your dog didn't have a relaxing time. You can also ask your horse what they feel about the person having them out on loan or the person who is responsible for their care at a livery yard. By understanding our animals' feelings, we can understand an awful lot.

The emotions may come from nowhere. You may suddenly find you're flooded with sadness, confusion or love. Sometimes the emotions pass through quickly – they are flashes of emotion. However you receive them, as long as you start your communication from a point of neutrality, you can be pretty sure the response came from your animal.

Sending emotion to your animal: In order to convey a message containing emotion successfully to your animal, you need to create those feelings clearly within yourself first. For instance, if you want to let your cat know that you're really unhappy with them dropping half-eaten mice on your head as you sleep, summon up strong feelings of disappointment or displeasure to communicate this to them.

Person type: A person who initially receives information from an animal via this mode could be someone who works in a caring setting, such as a therapist, social worker, nurse, counsellor or animal rescue worker, or someone who is comfortable about expressing their own emotions or having someone to express their emotions to them. People who might struggle with this one are those who have been emotionally hurt and tend to keep their heart and emotions well-hidden or protected. There is an exception: people who have been hurt are often much more heart-open to animals and empathic towards them than they are towards the species that caused them pain.

Physical sensations

You can also receive physical feelings – sensations. This is a fantastic mode of exchange and I encourage you to develop it as part of your animal communication toolkit.

Receiving sensations from your animal: You may ask your animal how they're feeling and have a flash of pain in your left foot, which would be the equivalent of their left hind paw or hoof. Or you may feel a strong dull ache in your stomach as they explain to you they're experiencing a stomach issue. Many animals complain about headaches (possibly the result of poor-quality food laden with additives and chemicals), so when you ask them how they feel, you may find you're experiencing a flash of pain in your own forehead.

The good news is that you don't 'own' these sensations. They don't stay with you, locked inside your own body for you to carry around. You log on to the frequency of the sensation, understand it and then allow it to pass through you. It's just a fleeting moment where an animal lets you know what they're feeling in their physical body.

Sending sensation to your animal: When you want to send a message using a physical sensation, you'll learn to imagine that feeling in your body first and then send it across to the animal. For example, you may wish to let your newly adopted rescue dog know that they're safe now. You need to send them a feeling of safety. To do this, make sure you're relaxed by taking a few deep breaths and then embody a sense of calm and peace. Using your intention, enlarge these feelings and let them expand out towards your dog. Your dog will sense these frequencies of peace and begin to relax and feel calm, as you give them a sense of being safe. This can be useful for any frightened animal you're trying to calm.

Some animals are extremely sensitive to physical sensations. It's said, for example, that a horse's entire body is as sensitive as our fingertips, which makes it possible for them to feel a fly on a single hair. The faces of crocodiles are covered with tiny bumps, containing nerve endings referred to as 'integumentary sensory organs', which are far more sensitive than our fingertips. Now I bet you didn't know that.

There's a great post on a Facebook group called We Love Elephants, which went viral.[9] It shows footage of a bull elephant charging at Alan McSmith, a South African guide. McSmith shows perfectly how calm energy can influence the behaviour of wild animals. Without any kind of physical contact, he settles the elephant by calmly holding his ground. Pachyderms are able to sense emotions such as fear and stress. When they sense calm energy, they feel the same. What this footage shows is that humans and animals are able to connect at a very deep level and, I believe, have far more in common than Joe Public realizes. McSmith goes on to say, 'Modern man still shares a kinship with the wild... In order to maintain our own respect and dignity, we must treat our environment in the same way.'

Person type: If you're aware of your body, rather than just moving it around without giving it much attention, then you may find this is your primary link of communication. Perhaps you are physically aware because you work out, practise yoga, run, swim, cycle or have an awareness of your posture. You don't have to be super-fit for this, thank goodness. In fact, I've found people who are physically impaired often have a heightened sense of their physicality and excel with this mode of communication. They're often quicker and more accurate than anyone else in the room.

Smell

I bet you could name quite a few species that love to have a good old sniff. Smell and taste are similar to each other and when you receive one you often receive the other too. If you struggle with this at the beginning, don't worry, you're not alone, you just need to practise having a sniff every day to hone your sense of smell.

Receiving smell from animals: This is the mode of communication that I was useless at for quite a while, then suddenly one day my olfactory receptors switched on. Now I live with a fox-poo-rollin'-lovin' dog, I want to switch them off again! I can be inside my car at traffic lights with all the windows up and smell cigarette smoke. I'll look around and two cars behind me there'll be someone smoking in their car, with all their windows up.

In spite of these inconveniences, if your animal goes missing, it's quite handy to ask them what smells they've come across. Perhaps they've passed a bonfire. It's also possible to receive acrid, flowery, musty, putrid, metallic or chemical smells from them.

Sending smell to animals: If you're concerned about what's causing your animal to scratch, you might want to recall the smell of your cleaning products as best you can and accompany the smell with the question: 'Is this causing you to scratch?' Your animal may be reacting to your fabric cleaner or what you use to wash the floor. Many animals complain about air fresheners, shampoos and plug-in scents.

Dogs possess up to 300 million olfactory receptors in their noses, compared to just 6 million in ours. Additionally, the part of a dog's brain dedicated to analysing smells is 40 times greater than our own. An indoor lavender plant can help calm a dog. A cat's sense of smell is about 14 times as strong as that of humans. Horses' sense of smell is greater than humans' and lesser than dogs'. Smell matters.

Person type: There is a handful of people who are really sensitive to smell and aware of it the moment they walk into a room, meet someone or attend an event. They just have a nose for it. However, we can all develop this sense by paying it more attention.

Taste

Taste – yum! Who doesn't love to eat good grub? Animals, some in particular, love to share their favourite tastes with us.

Receiving taste from animals: You can ask your cat, 'What's your favourite food?' and find yourself experiencing the taste of that delicacy. I've asked a cat this question and found myself biting into the flesh of a mouse and crunching on its bones with metaphorical blood trickling down my chin. Of course, I'm not *really* eating the mouse, but at that moment I'm enjoying it with just as much pleasure as the cat experiences. I've also asked a dog about their favourite food and found myself gnawing down on a sliver of tripe stick. And if you know about tripe stick, you'll know it's the stinkiest, most revolting dog treat on Earth (well, one of them).

Dogs have about 1,706 taste buds, compared to our 9,000 taste buds, which leaves them with a palate six times *inferior* to ours. Smell matters to dogs more than taste. If it smells good to your dog, they'll probably end up eating it. So it's helpful to put aside any revulsion you have about 'eating' foods your animal enjoys, because one day this might save their life. If your animal gets really ill and tells you it's because of something they've eaten, it could really help your vet, who will often ask, 'Do you know if they've eaten something?' The taste of a hard rubber squash ball could make all the difference between 'Wait and see' and an X-ray followed by life-saving surgery to remove it.

What's also interesting about dogs and cats is that they have taste buds tuned for water, which we don't have. This taste sense is found at the tip of the dog's or cat's tongue, which is the part of the tongue that they curl to lap water.

Sending taste to animals: To send taste to an animal, recall it as strongly as you can using your memory of it, or your imagination, then, using your intention, send the taste along with the question you want to ask about it. For instance, imagine the taste of chocolate and ask your sick dog, 'Did you eat something that tastes like this?'

Person type: The people who mainly communicate with animals this way are those who get a lot of pleasure out of the different tastes of food or who react badly to certain tastes. For most of us, though food is quite easy to eat, really tasting its flavours is quite another ball game. Next time you eat, practise naming the flavours in your food as well as the texture and how it makes you feel. Is it sweet, sour, bitter, salty or savoury? Smooth or crunchy? Does it make you drool with delight?

One more way to receive – gut knowing

Now that you've heard how the lining of your gut is really a 'second brain' with more neurons than your spinal cord, you'll understand why you often notice a feeling in that area of your body. When teaching, I often hear people declare, 'I just know,' and see them placing their hands on their stomach. That will be a gut knowing. And they're sensing it without any effort whatsoever. How lovely is that?! If you decide to accompany me on one of my cetacean retreats, you'll find it's the same when you're communicating with dolphins – effortless!

Signature frequency

> *'If you want to find the secrets of the universe, think in terms of energy, frequency and vibration.'*
> NIKOLA TESLA, INVENTOR

Tesla said it. Einstein agreed. Science proved it. Everything is made up of energy vibrating at different frequencies that can be measured (in Hertz), including our own bodies and the bodies of animals. Sound is everywhere. It's a universal language.

Elaine Thompson of Sound Therapy UK says, 'Friction and movement create sound, and as your body moves and your mind thinks, it resonates inside with sounds generated by your physical and chemical makeup. When you start to examine the really small details, all your body chemicals, muscles and organs have their own precise and specific frequency, and so does every virus and bacteria.'[10]

When a frequency moves through a medium like water, air or sand, it impacts it. The work of Dr Masaru Emoto demonstrates the effect of intentions on water. For example, when viewing water under a microscope, if you say to it, 'I love you,' it will form a beautiful snowflake shape, but if you say, 'I hate you,' it becomes gnarled and loses its structure.[11] This is yet another reason why talking kindly and compassionately to animals (and humans) can have such a healing effect on them. We mustn't forget that our human bodies are about 65 per cent water, so intentions do affect us.

When we communicate with an animal, we're logging on to that animal's unique signature frequency. It's a bit like their fingerprint. It's what makes the black cat we wish to communicate with different from a similar black cat. We're not accessing this frequency with fancy machinery and wires; we're employing our intention to connect with the animal's signature frequency and exchanging transmissions on the frequency of love.

You know, that reads like a much more complicated process than it actually is. Trust me, it's a very simple technique, and I'll lay it all out for you in Part II. I just wanted to share some background details here because I know you'll be bursting with questions once you start.

Frequencies matter

> *'What we have called matter is energy, whose vibrations have been lowered as to be perceptible to the senses. There is no matter.'*
> Albert Einstein, theoretical physicist

So we've learned that we're not solid, we're actually pockets of pulsating power. We're literally pockets of pulsating power that vibrate so slowly that we appear as matter – human beings, dogs, cats, guinea pigs or budgies.

Emotional frequencies

Emotions have individual frequencies too. I want to highlight a few of them to you. The lowest frequency is shame at 20 Hz. Guilt is 30 Hz, grief 75 Hz, courage 200 Hz, neutrality 250 Hz, acceptance 350 Hz, love 500 Hz, joy 540 Hz, peace 600 Hz and enlightenment 700–100 Hz.

If you're feeling shame or guilt, i.e. are at the lower end of the spectrum, you'll be experiencing what are called alpha frequencies of contraction. If you're feeling peace and joy at the higher end, you'll be experiencing expansion at the omega end of the scale:

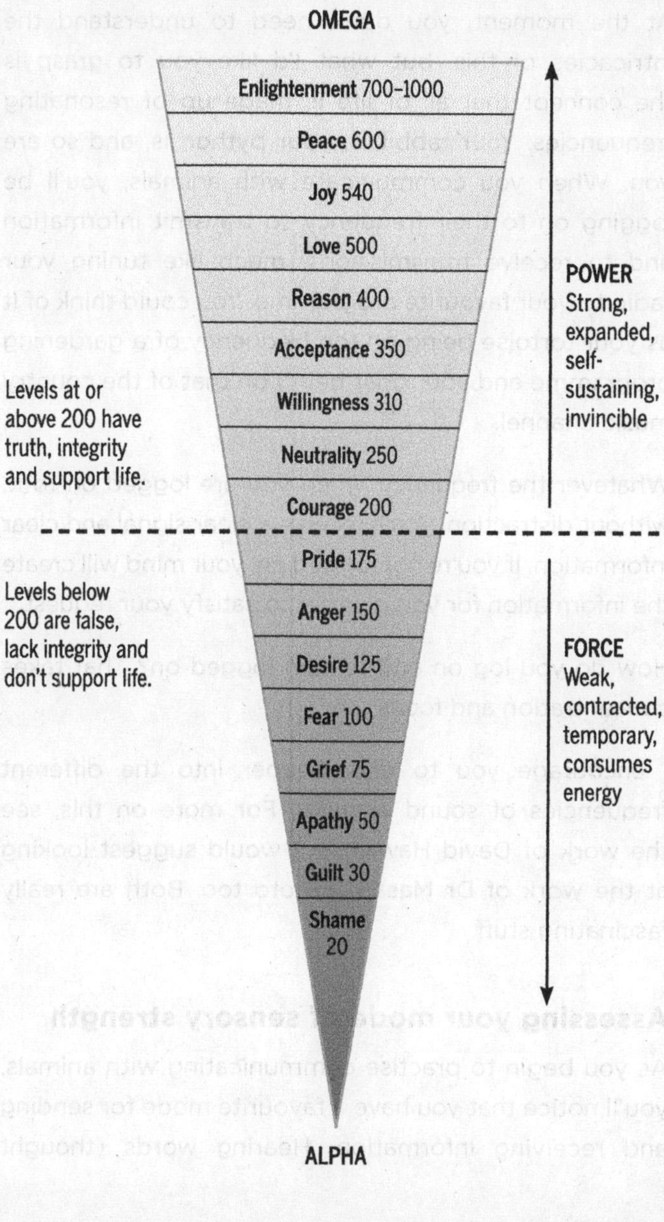
OMEGA
Enlightenment 700–1000
Peace 600
Joy 540
Love 500
Reason 400
Acceptance 350
Willingness 310
Neutrality 250
Courage 200
Pride 175
Anger 150
Desire 125
Fear 100
Grief 75
Apathy 50
Guilt 30
Shame 20
ALPHA
Levels at or above 200 have truth, integrity and support life.
Levels below 200 are false, lack integrity and don't support life.
POWER
Strong, expanded, self-sustaining, invincible
FORCE
Weak, contracted, temporary, consumes energy

At the moment, you don't need to understand the intricacies of this, but what I'd like you to grasp is the concept that all of life is made up of resonating frequencies. Your rabbit is, your python is, and so are you. When you communicate with animals, you'll be logging on to their frequency to transmit information and to receive transmissions, much like tuning your radio to your favourite programme. You could think of it as your tortoise being on the frequency of a gardening programme and your goat being on that of the country music channel.

Whatever the frequency, when you are logged on to it, without distraction, you'll receive a clear signal and clear information. If you're not logged on, your mind will create the information for you in order to satisfy your request.

How do you log on and remain logged on? That takes concentration and focus.

I encourage you to dive deeper into the different frequencies of sound analysis. For more on this, see the work of David Hawkins.[12] I would suggest looking at the work of Dr Masaru Emoto too. Both are really fascinating stuff.

Assessing your mode of sensory strength

As you begin to practise communicating with animals, you'll notice that you have a favourite mode for sending and receiving information. Hearing words (thought forms) is my favourite method, but, as it happens, I've had 15 years' training in listening. As a stage manager, I spent time in the rehearsal room sitting in silence, listening to the actors and director; then in the theatre, I spent more time listening to the creative team for direction or to the actors in order to cue the lighting or sound. That's a pretty solid training in listening.

I suggest you play with all the modes and strengthen them with practice so that you have the entire repertoire at your disposal. This will help you become more precise with the details and therefore more accurate in your communications.

The following two exercises will help you prepare for learning to communicate. Please don't skip them. They take very little time and will benefit you later on.

Exercise: Beyond planet Earth

This exercise helps you to unleash your mind and flex your intuitive muscle with creativity that ignites the imagination. It is particularly useful for people who have a profession that involves very left-hemisphere based thinking: logical, analytical, scientific. It helps balance the scales with right-hemisphere based thinking: imaginative, creative, intuitive.

Left-brain hemisphere	Right-brain hemisphere
Logical	Creative
Analytical	Intuitive
Precise	Artistic
Realistic	Visual
Fan of 'to do' lists	Does not like to follow directions
Likes things done sequentially	Is able to see the big picture
Makes decisions based on reality	Makes decisions based on emotion
Verbal communication	Non-verbal communication
Likes routine, sameness	Likes newness, novelty
Excels at science and maths	Excels at art and music
Facts	Feelings
Thinks in words	Visualizes
Computation	Daydreaming

The point of this exercise is for you to practise being imaginative so that you are more in tune with being intuitive. The writing and language will satisfy your left brain, and the creativity and imagination will satisfy your right brain, bringing beautiful balance. Bam!

You can do this exercise by writing it out or by recording it on your phone.

- Find a notepad and pen or have your phone at hand and ready to record (voice memo). Of course, you don't have to record it, but I find it helps to have that accountability, and you might like to listen to your wonderful creation afterwards.
- Imagine that you are leaving planet Earth and going somewhere far away.

- Now begin a story and incorporate as many wildly imaginative aspects as possible. Here's a short example of one I just devised.

  When I fly into the centre of the third pink planet, I often encounter dooleysquats. They are extremely friendly, but if you forget to kiss their tail in greeting they can get mightily upset and release a horrendous smell. What's most fun about the dooleysquats is the squeaky sound they make.

Okay, I know it sounds nuts, but that's the whole point. I don't want it to be logical, real or grounded. Use your imagination and go wild. If you're doing it right, you'll find you start laughing. Because it sounds crazy, right? I love it and hope you will too. Repeat as often as you need to – daily, weekly, whatever works until you find it's easy and comfortable to be so imaginative.

Here's another exercise to prepare you for animal communication.

Exercise: Tune in your senses

One of the simplest exercises to start tuning in to your senses is to put all your focus on one sense at a time. I prefer to do this outside in a location I'm not familiar with, but if that's not possible, anywhere outside or inside will do. It only takes about 10 minutes. You can record the details on your phone, then count them back afterwards.

- Sit or stand outside, whatever's more comfortable for you.
- Close your eyes and take a few deep relaxing breaths.

- *Hear sounds:* Focus on everything you can *hear*. Mentally make a list of 20 or more sounds. Be specific. This is crucial. Detail will help you hone your senses. For instance, rather than noting you can hear a car, note that the car is moving, its direction, its speed, the sound it makes as it accelerates or brakes. Do the same with birds. Don't just note that you hear birds, note the sound of the birds, their distance from you, the direction they're moving in and how many you think you hear.

- *Feel sensations:* Then move on to *physical sensations*, like the sun warming the left side of your body, your hair making your cheek tingle as the breeze gently moves it across your face, the temperature of your hands or the ache in your lower back. Note at least 20 physical sensations.

- *Feel emotions:* Move on to the *emotions* you are feeling. How does it feel to be in your environment, with the sun on your skin? How are you feeling personally about yourself? How are you feeling about work, play, adventure, travel? Do you need silence and solitude? Do you need to be sociable with friends? Tune in to your emotional landscape at this moment.

- *Smell:* Next try and note as many *smells* as possible. Breathe in through your nose and try to put a name to them: exhaust fumes, manure, the scent of lavender... You could even smell your own body odour. Eek!

- *Taste:* Then move on to what you can *taste*. First note everything you can taste within your mouth, like stale coffee or the remnants of the morning muffin. Then breathe in through your mouth and see if you can add a few more tastes, like the taste of damp air, cigarette smoke, grass or earth. I know this is a harder one, and very linked in with smell, but give it a go anyway. You might surprise yourself.

- *See:* Now open your eyes and note everything you can see. Remember to be detailed. Noting 'trees' is just plain lazy. Where are they in relation to you? How many of them are there? Do you know what type they are? Are they still or are their branches moving in the wind? Can you see animals? What are they doing? Are they travelling or still? If they are moving, what direction are they moving in and at what speed? Notice things far away as well as close up, and put in all the descriptive detail you can. This has got to be the easiest sense because humans are so driven by sight, so note 20 plus sights in as much detail as you can.

We're now going to move into the next part, where you'll learn preparation, connection and effective steps to communicating with animals. Excited? Come on then, I'm waiting for ya!

SUMMARY

- Intuition is very real.
- You may be a sensoric personality type or an intuitive personality type. Your personality type will determine how easily you learn animal communication.
- You can always strengthen your intuition.

- Everything is frequency. When you communicate with an animal, you're logging on to its unique signature frequency.
- Honing your senses will help you to use all the modes of communication.

Part II

GETTING STARTED WITH THE HEART-TO-HEART METHOD

'Take the first step in faith. You don't have to see the whole staircase, just take the first step.'

MARTIN LUTHER KING, MINISTER

Chapter 4

Preparation

'In all things success depends on previous preparation, and without such previous preparation there is sure to be failure.'
CONFUCIUS, PHILOSOPHER

Preparation is key to shifting from a busy life and high expectations to being present, relaxed, open and calm. The Heart-to-Heart method of preparation involves five steps that show you how to prepare in order to communicate effectively with animals and explain why it will be a problem if you don't prepare. Each step builds upon the previous one and teaches you how to get into the right mindset *before* reaching out to communicate with animals.

It's tempting to jump straight into communicating. Yet there are no shortcuts to real success. Preparation is something I wish I'd spent more time on when I first started out. Look at it this way: a 100-year-old tree starts off as a tiny seed. You sow the seed, give it a light dusting of soil and gently water it, then, with sunshine and rain, it grows slowly into the seedling stage and on into the sapling stage. Over time, your tiny seed becomes a tall, strong and stable tree, but it takes patience and nurturing to get it to grow to its full capacity. As does animal communication.

So, we'll focus now on relaxing the body, calming the mind and moving forward through a simple self-body scan, a grounding meditation and heart-opening process. Then you'll practise your first communication exercise at the end of the chapter.

Step 1: Deep relaxation technique

> *'You have enough. You do enough. You are enough. Relax.'*
>
> Anonymous

A relaxation practice can have many benefits, including lowering blood pressure, slowing the heart and breathing rate, reducing stress hormones and muscle tension, and improving sleep quality, mood and concentration. If you recognize that you're an anxious person or have been anxious for a while, a regular relaxation practice will help your body get used to being relaxed.

Did you know that when we are anxious, we overbreathe and our body becomes short of carbon dioxide? The result is that the sympathetic part of our nervous system goes on red alert and our body prepares for the fight or flight response. Imagine now that you're your cat or dog and this highly alert human wants to connect with you. If I were your animal, I'd turn and walk in the opposite direction.

Regularly throughout your animal communication practice it's good to imagine yourself in your animal's paws and consider, 'How would I feel if...?' Wouldn't you much rather your human was relaxed and at ease? That's the kind of person I'd want to connect with if I was given the choice.

For all of the reasons above, committing to a deep body relaxation as part of your preparation to communicate with animals is a win-win. Don't try too hard. Just allow the relaxation to happen without forcing it. Take things slowly.

Exercise: Deep relaxation technique

Preparation

- Find a quiet, warm place where you won't be disturbed.
- Wear loose clothing.
- Sit in a supportive chair with your hands resting loosely in your lap.
- Uncross your legs.
- Support your spine with a cushion if you need it.

Intention

- Begin with three deep slow breaths and hold the intention of relaxing.

Forehead

- Bring your focus to your forehead. As you breathe in, create furrows of tension in your brow. As you breathe out, relax your forehead, releasing any tension in your face.

Mouth

- Take a slow breath in, and as you breathe out, relax your tongue, allowing it to fall away from the roof of your mouth.

Jaw

- Take a slow breath in and send the breath into your jaw as you exhale to the word 'relax'.
- Release any tension in your jaw.
- Continue to breathe in through your nose and exhale 'relax' into your jaw.
- Feel your jaw relaxing.
- Breathe in slowly, pause and then breathe out slowly.

Neck

- Take a slow breath in and send the breath into your neck as you exhale to 'relax'.
- Feel your neck loosening.
- Continue to breathe in through your nose and exhale 'relax' into your neck.
- Breathe in slowly, pause and then breathe out slowly.

Throat

- Take a slow breath in and send the breath into your throat as you exhale to 'relax'.
- Release any tension in your throat.
- Continue to breathe in through your nose and exhale 'relax' down your throat.
- Breathe in slowly, pause and then breathe out slowly.

Shoulders

- Take a slow breath in and send the breath to your shoulders as you exhale to 'relax'.
- Feel your shoulders growing heavier.
- Continue to breathe in through your nose and exhale 'relax' down to your shoulders.
- Observe your shoulders sinking down and relaxing.

Arms

- Take a slow breath in and send the breath down your arms as you exhale to 'relax'.
- Feel your arms growing heavier.
- Feel your hands resting in your lap growing heavier.
- Continue to breathe in through your nose and exhale 'relax' down your arms and into your hands.
- Breathe in slowly, pause and then breathe out slowly.

Stomach and intestines

- Breathe in slowly and send the breath down to your stomach and intestines as you exhale to 'relax'.
- Observe whether your stomach is clenched or relaxed.
- Breathe in, pause, breathe out and relax your stomach and intestines.
- Repeat: breathe in, pause, breathe out and relax your stomach and intestines. Take your time. Nice and easy. Breathe in slowly, pause and then breathe out slowly.

Spine

- Take a slow breath in and send the breath down your spine from your neck to your tailbone as you exhale to 'relax'.
- Breathe in, pause, breathe out and relax your spine.
- Repeat: breathe in, pause, breathe out and relax your spine.
- Observe how your back is in contact with the chair or cushion supporting you.

Hips and buttocks

- Take a slow breath in and send the breath down to your hips and buttocks as you exhale to 'relax'.
- Feel your hips relaxing and your buttocks sinking heavily into the seat of the chair.
- Take your time. Breathe in slowly and then breathe out slowly.
- Observe your lower body feeling heavier than before as the tension begins to leave you.

Legs

- Continue to breathe in through your nose and now send the breath down to your legs as you exhale to 'relax'.
- Feel your legs growing heavier.
- Feel how the backs of your thighs are in contact with the seat of the chair.
- Continue to breathe in through your nose and exhale 'relax' into your legs.
- Observe where you may be holding tension and breathe into those areas.

Feet

- Begin by closing your eyes and shutting yourself off from external stimulation.
- Focus on your feet resting comfortably on the ground.
- Notice the connection with the floor beneath you.
- If you prefer, remove your shoes and socks and feel your skin in contact with the ground.
- Spend a moment breathing in through your nose and imagining guiding the air down inside your body to your feet.
- With every out-breath, send the breath down to your feet and silently voice in your mind the word 'relax'.
- Feel your feet growing heavier and more connected to the ground.

Whole body

- Imagine your whole body entering a deep and relaxed state.
- You are feeling deeply relaxed.
- Take a few more slow breaths and then open your eyes.
- Observe the changes in how you feel and breathe.

By placing your focus on your body as you go through relaxing parts of it, you turn your mind away from tension and become more centred.

Try relaxing for 10 minutes every other day, then build it up to 20 minutes. If this feels like too big of a commitment, just remember how much time you could be wasting feeling anxious or angry each day. Remember, too, it's much more agreeable to communicate with someone who is relaxed rather than someone who is tense.

Relaxation techniques are skills, and your ability to relax will improve with practice. Make the time and please be patient with yourself.

Step 2: CalmSpace

'The ideal of calm exists in a sitting cat.'

Jules Renard, author

Many of us live with a level of persistent low-grade stress. Sadly, it's a common daily experience that has become normal and much of the time we don't even recognize it's there. Although there may be no obvious signs of stress, the hormone called cortisol, which is linked with stress, grinds down our mental and physical health over time. So you can help yourself *and* your communication with animals (because both are inextricably linked) by making time to clear your mind and bring calm into your life.

Five CalmSpace methods

Here are a few suggestions to get you started:

1. Meditation

Meditation allows you to take charge of your own nervous system and emotions. It's very empowering. It can help resolve the physical and emotional effects of stress and increase your ability to relax. Consider meditation a spring clean for the mind, resulting in a mind without agitation. Call it mental hygiene. It also helps you to concentrate and to be centred and focused, so you'll become less and less distracted. Another fantastic consequence of meditation is that it helps you to reconnect with your inner life through silence and you discover your inner voice.

2. Move your body

Be it walking, dancing, surfing, yoga or *tai chi*, 15 minutes of activity helps get the endorphins, or feel-good hormones, pumping and helps to clear the mind. Activity also improves your ability to cope with stress, release tension and enhance positive thinking. It can help you feel better and stay calmer. Stationary = stagnant. Active = achievement.

3. Just one thing

Not every task is urgent. The easiest way to get your mind out of an overwhelm inactivity trance is to create achievable momentum. That's why the 'just one thing' mantra is such a powerful tool for your toolkit. By engaging in *just one thing* from this chapter, you're taking positive action.

4. Change your setting

A simple change of surroundings can be the perfect break. Go outside for a few minutes and tilt your face towards the sunshine. By changing your physical perspective on things, you can often find new ways of approaching difficulties, and nature has a wonderful way of putting us back into a positive frame of mind. Do this before a communication if you're feeling a bit stuck.

5. And ... breathe

There is a direct connection between our emotional state and breathing. An anxious, overwhelmed or frustrated person will breathe faster than someone who is relaxed and calm. It's quite nice to add in an affirmation as a focus for your mind. Affirmations are anything we say or think. They can be short sentences intended to influence the conscious and unconscious mind. I love them. Try silently saying 'I am' on your in-breath and 'Calm' on your out-breath. An alternative could be to inhale with 'I am' and exhale with 'Relaxed.' Focus on deep, slow and steady breaths to bring your heart rate down and shift your emotional state.

Exercise: Five breaths

Try this now:

- Take a slow, deep breath in through your nose over a count of five, filling your lungs with air.
- Hold your breath for a count of five and then slowly release the air through your mouth over a count of five.
- Repeat the sequence five times.

Do you notice your feelings shift? Has your frustration or anxiety dissolved? Do you feel calmer and more relaxed?

Step 3: The body sweep

Before you begin communicating with an animal, it's vital to have a quick check in with your own body. This way you can be clearer about any physical sensations you receive and not confuse them with your own aches and pains.

It's a simple sweep of the body starting from the head and working down to the feet. There's no judgement or adjustment needed, just an awareness of what you are experiencing prior to starting communication. If you do discover areas of concern, you can choose to send your breath to the parts that are tense or painful as a form of self-healing.

Exercise: The body sweep

During your sweep notice any discomfort, stickiness, colours or emotions that come to you. Make a mental note of these for later.

- Sit or stand where you won't be disturbed. Close your eyes and take three relaxing breaths.
- Begin by moving your awareness to the top of your head, then bring it down the front of your face, noticing how your forehead feels, how your eyes feel, and your tongue, lips and jaw feel.
- Now go behind your head and down your neck and slowly into your shoulders. Observe how you are holding your neck, whether there is any pain there, and whether your shoulders are hunched and tense (they shouldn't be if you've done the Deep Relaxation Technique, or relaxed your shoulders down from your ears).
- Check your throat. Swallow and see how that feels. Is it easy and free or sore and blocked?
- Bring your awareness into your chest and observe your lungs as you breathe, then observe your heart and how you feel emotionally. What is your mood? Do you need to dedicate more time to CalmSpace?
- Move down into your stomach and then down into your intestines. How does your stomach feel? Bloated, full, nicely

satisfied or hungry? How is your digestion? Are you eating the foods your body needs to support a healthy digestion?

- Return to your left shoulder and work down your left arm towards your hand. As you sweep, observe the muscles and joints along the way. When you reach your left hand, rest there for a moment, observing how your palm and fingers are feeling.
- Return to your right shoulder and work down your right arm towards your hand. As you sweep, observe the muscles and joints along the way. When you reach your right hand, rest there for a moment, observing how your palm and fingers are feeling.
- Next sweep down your spine and into your hips, observing any area that flags itself up to you with pain, colour, stickiness or simply a feeling that things aren't fully functioning.
- Move into your left hip and work down your left leg towards your foot. As you sweep, observe the muscles and joints along the way. When you reach your left foot, rest there for a moment, observing how your sole and toes are feeling.
- Move into your right hip and work down your right leg towards your foot. As you sweep, observe the muscles and joints along the way. When you reach your right foot, rest there for a moment, observing how your sole and toes are feeling.
- From the base of your feet, take a mental sweep upwards through your body, reminding yourself of any areas that flagged themselves up as out of balance.
- When you reach the top of your head, take a long deep breath and exhale slowly.
- Now take a notepad and make a note of all the areas that flagged themselves up for you during your body sweep.

Step 4: Get grounded

'Keep a tree in your heart and perhaps the singing bird will come.'

CHINESE PROVERB

Getting grounded means having a greater awareness of your connection with the Earth. Animals are very grounded, including the ones in the ocean and the air. They are unburdened by income and achievement, instead focusing on survival, procreation and joy. They live in the moment and in connection with the energy of the Earth, sun and moon. Some species use their connection with Earth energy in order to navigate thousands of miles for food or to give birth during a full moon.

I've observed that when a person is feeling grounded, animals are keener to connect with them. The person feels like a safe harbour in a storm, a place to retreat to, providing shelter and warmth. I can't stress enough how much it will help your animal communication to spend time on getting yourself into a good place mentally, emotionally and physically. It's not a selfish act; it's vital for long-term accuracy and effectiveness. All of this prep will become second nature to you if you practise it over time.

The following meditation can be very helpful for anyone without regular contact with nature. If you're not feeling particularly grounded, this is also a great step for you to take prior to connecting with the animals you love.

Meditation: The tree

Sit comfortably with your back straight but relaxed and your hands in your lap.

Ready now, close your eyes and take a long deep breath.

As you exhale, notice how your body is sinking into a relaxed state.

Bring your attention to your breath. Keep your focus on your out-breath and observe your breath leaving you.

Continue to focus on your out-breath and allow your breath to move gently away.

Before you breathe in, you'll notice a pause.

Continue to focus on every out-breath. Be in the present moment. Allow your breath to come and go without force, in a relaxed way.

Imagine that you are sitting with your back up against a large tree. Feel the bark behind your back, rough or smooth. Notice the smell of the tree. Observe the branches and leaves.

Relax back into the tree and notice how it supports you – so strong and steady.

Relax back even further and find that you are merging with the tree. You and the tree are becoming one.

Your back is strong like the trunk of the tree. Feel the solidness keeping you upright.

Your branches are extending out from your head and upper body.

Observe the roots of the tree going down into the Earth from your lower body. These are your roots. They go deeper and deeper into the Earth and grow wider and wider.

Now take hold of the Earth with your roots and feel how it comes up to hold you.

Imagine pulling the Earth energy into your roots. It will nourish you and replenish your energy.

Imagine sinking your hands into the Earth. Touch the warm Earth and feel her energy.

Pull that Earth energy up your roots and into your trunk, then up into your branches and watch it enter your leaves.

Now breathe that Earth energy up your roots into your trunk, then your branches and then your leaves.

Feel the gravitational pull of the Earth holding you.

Hold your hands up and away from your body like the branches of your tree and feel the warmth of the sun beaming down upon you, warming your hands, your branches and leaves, and giving you life.

Feel the sun energy flowing into your body.

Notice how more connected you feel with the nourishing energy of the Earth beneath you and the life-force of the sun above.

The connection to the Earth helps you to remain grounded.

Sink deeper and deeper into a calm space.

At one with the tree.

You are the tree.

Your roots are supported by the Earth and your branches are nurtured by the sun.

Take a moment to record this feeling. It will help you return to this state of being.

Now bring your awareness back to your breath.

Notice the out-breath and how it fades away.

Breathe slowly, to your own rhythm.

Take a slow, deep breath, and when you are ready un-merge, then bring your awareness back to the space you are in.

Take another slow, deep breath, and when you feel ready, gently open your eyes.

Step 5: The open heart

> *'The heart has eyes which the brain knows nothing of.'*
>
> Charles H. Perkhurst, clergyman and social reformer

When we communicate with animals, we come from our heart with an intention of unconditional love. One of the reasons people struggle to connect with animals is because they have closed their heart, and sometimes bolted and padlocked it as well. In some cases this has happened in childhood and in others more recently. Spiritually, if your heart is closed or blocked, you may experience a lack of empathy or a feeling of disconnection. You may not trust yourself and lack self-esteem. There can also be deep insecurity and an ever-present sense of fear. All in all, it can be harder to communicate.

Yet the feelings of grief, anger, jealousy or hatred are often what draw people to animals in the first place. Animals express such a vast amount of unconditional love that it feels good to be in their presence. They are literally healing us by their be-ingness. So that we can hear them, and not just be healed *by* them, we need to spend some time working towards healing our own heart, one gentle step at a time.

When our heart is open, we naturally feel love and compassion for others and are open to receiving. Opening the heart is the start of a healing process and key to clear communication with animals.

Exercise: The OpenHeart process

A simple yet profound way to open the heart and raise self-esteem is by visual cues or affirmations. I invite you to write an affirmation on a sticky note and strategically position it as a daily reminder to yourself. Make as many as you like – the more, the merrier. These statements help to increase positivity for your heart. You can stick them on your fridge door, laptop or bathroom mirror. Stick them on your forehead, for all I care, just stick them somewhere!

I'm going to suggest some affirmations for you, but really I want you to create your own, because they'll hold much more power coming from you.

- 'I am opening to love.'
- 'I forgive myself.'
- 'I deeply and completely love and accept myself.'
- 'I live in balance.'
- 'I respect myself.'

You can also say the affirmations out loud and make some up at random times throughout the day: when you're on the bus, taking lunch or having a bath. Be creative and spontaneous. I'm not suggesting you shout them out loud on the bus, but if you want to, go for it, others might benefit!

- 'I take loving care of myself.'
- 'I am whole and complete.'
- 'I am beautiful.'
- 'I feel peace, love and joy.'
- 'I am healthy and energized.'

Affirmations are about shifting energy to a different vibration – a more positive one. You can say them to attract what you want in your world. When you first say them, they won't feel true, because if they were, you wouldn't need to say them in the first place. But it's like planting seeds - it takes some time from the first planting to the blossoming of the rose.

Make your affirmations with faith and feeling and believe that they have already been fulfilled. Louise Hay, the founder of this book's publishing company, Hay House, and the queen of affirmations, produced many affirmation oracle cards that you might enjoy.

Your first communication practice

I bet by now you're keen to get going. Wait no more. In this exercise you'll learn how to move your awareness, your consciousness, from your body into the body of an animal with whom you want to communicate. That might sound challenging, but really it can be a lot of fun, and what you'll experience can be astounding. Just focus on enjoying the experience and don't think about the results. Be in the moment.

This exercise also opens your mind and encourages your consciousness to embrace new possibilities. Let go of any preconceptions you may have. The best way to approach this exercise is with a light-hearted sense of fun.

Exercise: Through their eyes

You can do this exercise with horse friends, bird buddies and all sorts of animals, but let's start with an animal you already know and love to bits.

- Find a quiet space to sit and relax. You don't need your animal in the room with you for this one, but if they're already close by, that's okay too.
- Think of an animal in your life now and mentally ask them, 'Can I merge with you and see things from your point of view?'
- If the response is positive or inviting, you know they've agreed.
- If you feel any resistance at all, understand that now may not be the best time for them. Waiting is not failure; it's a respectful acknowledgement of your animal's wishes and can also be a reflection on your state of being. Give it a few hours or a few days. Practise the Deep Relaxation Technique or CalmSpace. Then ask again. When they agree, continue with the following steps.

Step 1

- Close your eyes and picture the animal in front of you.
- Try and visualize, as best you can, their face and features. Notice the length of their whiskers, the size of their paws or the shine of their long, lustrous mane.
- See them standing, perching or sprawled out in front of you and say to them, 'Thank you for being with me.'
- If you're not a particularly visual kind of person, don't worry. Instead imagine that they're there with you and remember how they look.

Step 2

- Imagine now that you're shrinking down into a tiny version of yourself, shrinking down into your chest area. You are becoming a much, much smaller version of yourself inside yourself, while your outer body is remaining where it is.

- To help you to retain the image of yourself inside yourself, transform it into the image of a dot of light or another image you can sustain, perhaps that of a fairy, unicorn or elf.

Step 3

- Float slowly up your chest into your neck and then into your head.
- At the top of your head there is a trapdoor. It can look any way you want it to. Be as creative as you like.
- Open the door, and now, as the tiny dot of light (or whatever image you have chosen), fly out of the top of your head and over to the top of your animal's head.
- They have a door at the top of their head too.
- Open your animal's door, slip inside and close the door behind you.
- Be open to your animal changing their mind and asking you to leave. Sometimes they find the sensation of your presence unusual and prefer it to be for a very short time only. If they ask you to leave, please honour their request immediately and exit back to your own body using the guidance in step 11.

Step 4

- Float down into your animal's chest area and allow them to get used to the feeling of you being there.
- You are now as one with your animal. You are your animal. When you ask them to do something, you'll be doing it as them inside their body while your body remains seated.

- Slowly glide up to their eyes and for the first time in your life look through their eyes. Amazing, isn't it? You'll have lost all sense of your own sense of sight and will be seeing things entirely differently, from their perspective.
- Notice what they can see and how they see it. Notice if you are close to the ground or high up with a panoramic view.

Step 5

- Now focus on their protective coat: the fur, hair, feathers or scales of your friend.
- How does it feel to be wearing their coat?
- What does it mean to them?

Step 6

- Ask your animal, 'What do you like to do for fun?'
- As your animal, allow yourself to do that fun thing. You could find yourself galloping across a field or flying across to your best friend to sit on their shoulder and nuzzle into their neck. Go with the flow and whatever you feel your animal wants you to experience.
- Notice how it feels to do this fun thing. Become aware of why your animal enjoys it so much.
- And be open. The reason they enjoy it may not be the one that you think.

Step 7

- Now picture your human standing in front of you and shouting at you or telling you off, saying words like 'Shut up!' or '*Will* you get *out* of my way?'

- As your animal, notice how you feel. What do you feel physically when someone you love talks harshly to you?

Step 8

- Now picture your human standing in front of you and saying words of adoration, like 'I *love* you. You're *so special*.'
- As your animal, notice how you feel. What do you feel physically when someone you love talks kindly to you?

Step 9

- Take a moment to let your animal know just how much they mean to you and why you're so grateful that they're in your life.

Step 10

- Ask them gently, 'Do you have a message or gift for me?'
- Openly receive whatever comes to you. It may be something physical like a crystal or box, or an emotion, an image or some words.
- Accept gratefully anything you receive and say, 'Thank you.'

Step 11

- Now prepare to leave your animal's body, knowing you can return whenever you are both willing.
- Say to them, 'I am going to leave your body now,' and float up to the top of their head.
- Open the trapdoor there, fly out and close the door behind you.
- Fly back to the top of your own head, slip inside and close the door at the top of your head.
- Glide down into your chest area.

- With your eyes closed, picture again your animal in front of you.
- Notice your perspective has changed and you're now viewing them from your seat.
- Again thank them. Say, 'Thank you for doing this exercise with me.'
- Gently dissolve the image of them before you and allow them to carry on with their business.

Step 12

- Bring your focus back to yourself and that tiny dot of light in your chest.
- Morph back into that tiny version of yourself.
- Expand outwards to fill every part of your body.
- Bring yourself back into your body awareness.
- Take a few seconds to move your fingers and toes.
- Take a slow deep breath and release it.
- When you feel you're fully back, gently open your eyes.

Step 13

You might like to make a note of everything you experienced:

- What you noticed when you looked out of your animal's eyes.
- How it felt to wear their coat.
- Your response to harsh words.
- Your response to kind words.
- And any message or gift your animal gave you. They gave it you with purpose. It's no accident you received what you did.

How was your experience with your animal? Did it take your mind outside the box? I understand some people feel they are making it all up. You do need to allow your imagination freedom.

If you feel it didn't work at all for you, please question if you were expecting too much, like something really solid and concrete, rather than going with the flow of whatever came to you. Even if we feel we know what our animal likes to do for fun, we can sometimes be surprised to find they wish to express something else. Be as neutral as possible, but also go with what you feel they are expressing, even if that is what you presumed it would be.

If you feel the exercise really isn't working as you were hoping, just go with the parts that are (if any) and know that you can always repeat it another day.

Some people prefer to close the door to their head when they fly out and over to their animal. They worry that by leaving it open they are open and vulnerable to some kind of negative attack. I hold no such fear and prefer to leave it open to remind myself to return. Whatever feels comfortable to you is okay. Like a lot of animal communication, it's about finding your own way and what works effectively for you and your mindset. The reason I close the door to the animal's head when I slip inside is because I know I'm going to be 'moving' as that animal and I struggle with the thought of their door flapping as I race through a tall grass meadow or roll in some wonderful fox poo!

Repeat the exercise as many times as you like if your animal is willing, because it will increase your connection with them and your ability to think outside the box. These aspects will strengthen your communication with all animals. Each time you practise this you're learning to get out of the way of your own preconceptions and to go with the flow of what your animal is expressing to you. Plus, your animal will love being able to show you the ropes. Animals enjoy being our teachers and encouraging willing, listening students.

A more expansive world is opening up to you. You're learning it's not three-dimensional after all. It's limitless, and what's more, you can access it.

SUMMARY

- Preparation is the foundation of animal communication. Take your time with it and adjust, depending upon how stressed or busy you're feeling.
- When you're relaxed, communication will flow more easily for you.
- When you're calm and grounded, animals will be more willing to connect with you.
- Body sweep before you communicate to understand the difference between your physical sensations and those of the animal.
- Find ways to be open-hearted towards animals.

Chapter 5

Making a Connection

'Our first teacher is our own heart.'

Cheyenne proverb

The Heart-to-Heart method of connecting with an animal can also be broken down into five steps. Yep, just five. Hoorah for simplicity. In this chapter, I'll walk you through each step one at a time. I'll then give you guidance on verifying questions you can ask a cat, dog or horse, which can be adapted to suit other species too. I'm also going to explain a straightforward practice of ending the communication with an animal.

Ways to approach communicating with an animal

There are two basic approaches to animal communication, and you can try them both and see which works better for you as you start out. After you've been practising over a few months, take a risk and try the opposite approach. You really want to have both methods in your toolkit to keep your animal communication as flexible and fluid as possible.

Face to face

You may decide you wish to practise your communication with the animal in front of you. Some people prefer this approach because they find it feels 'normal' and familiar. But, hey, watch out for trip wires. When animals look away, yawn, move away or go to sleep, it's quite easy to jump to the same conclusion that you would with human-to-human communication and assume they're not interested. But this could be a mistake. Over the years animals have demonstrated to thousands of students the fact that they're not looking at them and seem to be paying no attention at all doesn't mean they're not engaged or communicating. It's possible to communicate with animals in the sea without seeing them face to face, so remain open-minded during your communications.

When communicating with animals face to face, please be sensitive to their comfort level. Some animals may feel uncomfortable if you look at them directly. In which case, have 'soft eyes' and glance sidewards or down so they can feel relaxed and safe. Think *soft and gentle*.

Via a photograph

Although it may seem strange, practising communication with an animal from their photograph can often be easier than having the animal present. The photograph remains in your hand or beside you the entire time and you're not going to be discouraged by the animal's behaviour. There is stillness to the experience and it's easier to maintain concentration.

I find that about 90 per cent of students find it easier communicating with animals from their photograph when they first start. Surprised? It's because they're able to maintain their focus; they can close their eyes to eliminate distractions, knowing that when they open them again the animal's image is right in front of them.

You're not communicating with the photograph; it's a pathway to the animal's energy - a prop, if you like, a link through to the animal's unique signature frequency.

I've summarized helpful photograph requirements for you:

Photograph requirements

- A clear view of the animal's eyes
- No light reflection/glare on their eyes
- No red eye
- Taken at their eye level
- Highly pixilated/high resolution (aim for 500kb or higher)
- Prey animals - a side, head and neck shot, plus a full-body shot

- Outside shots in natural lighting work well
- Only one animal in the picture
- No people (especially not on a horse)
- No rug/coat on a horse; preferably no tack at all

If the animal has cataracts or is blind, or is missing one or both eyes, you can still communicate with them. Communicate from a clear high-resolution photo of their face and body. Sometimes it's helpful to have a couple to choose from.

Now breathe.

The Heart-to-Heart method

The undervalued breath

You probably rarely think about breathing. It's an unconscious act that we only tend to observe when it becomes a focus, e.g. during a bad cold, snorkelling or when finding ourselves out of breath.

During this first step I will ask you to breathe in through your nose and out of the mouth for a very good reason – you have to concentrate on this and be aware of it, and so your attention is brought into the present moment.

If you prefer to breathe in and out through your nose and feel you can still bring your full attention to the present moment that way, go with that. But if you find you need more help to let go of racing thoughts and to feel calm, do try the nose and mouth technique. Over time you'll discover which technique is more helpful to your animal communication.

Your best communication environment

Think about the best place for you to practise communicating with animals. In the beginning it helps to find somewhere that you find comfortable and nurturing and that will remain peaceful and quiet.

Turn off all your devices. Have a pad and pen beside you, ready to note any information the animal shares. You can enhance your environment with candles, incense and pictures of your animals. You may like to place a colourful scarf around your shoulders or a blanket over your legs. These physical cues can be helpful over time because they become ingrained reminders to the emotional, mental and physical body that you are now moving into your *still-point* and preparing yourself for communication with animals. Then each time you practise, you may find it easier to just be and communicate.

Step 1: Connect to the breath (relaxed, calm still-point)

- Sit comfortably with your eyes closed, back straight, feet flat on the floor and your palms resting in your lap.

- Place all of your focus on your breathing.
- Take a slow breath in through your nose and breathe out slowly through your mouth.
- Take another slow breath in through your nose and breathe out slowly through your mouth.
- This time take a slow breath in through your nose, pause, and breathe out slowly through your mouth.
- Keep with this breathing in your own natural rhythm.
- Add the words 'I am' on your in-breath and 'calm' on your out-breath.
- Scan your body for any tension or tight spots and use your intention to 'breathe' into those areas while relaxing more deeply on every out-breath.
- Feel your body releasing any tension.
- Breathe in, pause, and breathe out, relaxing more deeply.
- Breathe in, pause, and breathe out, relaxing more deeply.
- Breathe in, pause, and breathe out, relaxing more deeply.
- Your body is feeling relaxed and softer now. Your awareness is more awake and alert. You're feeling calm and peaceful. This is perfect. This is your *still-point*.

How long you need for this step often depends on how agitated things have been in your life and how easy it is for you to transform your mood into calm, relaxed alertness. But if you've prepared well with the techniques and processes in the last chapter, you'll find this is easy for you. Cherish this time to nurture yourself and surrender to stillness before moving on.

Step 2: Anchor in the heart (open your heart)

- Drop your awareness down into your heart area and rest there. This doesn't need to be the actual bloody and beating heart – you don't have to get literal about it. The general heart area will be just fine.
- Connect with your love for animals. Think of an animal you love and adore or a species that you admire. This will automatically trigger the frequency of love.
- Rest in that sanctuary of love.
- If you wish to connect with your own animal, remind yourself why you love them so much. Recall all the happy moments you've experienced together.
- If you wish to communicate with an animal you don't know, it's just as important to anchor in the frequency of love by placing all of your focus there and reminding yourself why you love or admire animals or why you want to make a difference to their lives.

- Imagine your heart is full to bursting with the fathoms of love you feel.
- Recognize that every wish to communicate with an animal needs to originate from a loving place. There is no space for judgement or criticism here.

You may notice that you feel more open-hearted and compassionate now. This is the place from where we communicate with all animals, helping them feel safe with us.

Step 3: Connect heart to heart (frequency connection)

- Using your intention, extend some of this love from your heart across to the heart area of the animal with whom you wish to communicate. (You need not concern yourself about the exact location of the animal's heart – the general vicinity will do. Intention is the key.) Trust that it reaches them, connecting you heart to heart, together on the frequency of love.
- If you are a visual person, picture your love as a soft beam of light reaching from you across to them and connecting heart to heart. The light beam can be any colour that resonates for you at the time.
- You are now connected heart to heart with the animal you're going to communicate with.

With your intention to communicate with the animal, you have logged on to their unique signature frequency. It's what makes them an individual. Now that you are connected, you may begin to see and feel impressions from the animal. That's all good. Make a note of them on a pad, then continue with the next steps.

Step 4: 'I love you' (foundation of communication)

- Silently in your mind, or out loud if you prefer, say to the animal: 'I love you' and their name, for example 'I love you, Texas.'
- Repeat it once or twice if you like.

We do this to let the animal know that we are coming to them in loving-kindness – that we are approaching from a place of unconditional love.

Whether this is your own animal, a friend's animal or an animal that's new to you, you can still declare your unconditional love to them before you enter into communication. There is an infinite amount of love to be shared.

Step 5: Greeting and intention (manners and mindset)

I feel manners work in a way that's two-fold: we expect our dogs to sit, stay and come when called, or our horses to keep us safe and not throw us off at the first sight of some spooky action at a distance; but also, to enhance and foster trust between species, we need to extend the same level of good feeling back to them. So I like to do a simple greeting before asking an animal some questions. It's a 'Hi, how ya' doing?' equivalent. We can tweak this step a little, depending upon the animal we're communicating with.

- Silently in your mind, or out loud if you prefer, say to the animal, 'Hi, my name is [insert name] and I'd like to talk with you.'
- Another option would be, 'Hi, my name is [insert name] and I'd like to communicate with you.'
- Alternatively, if you know the animal, 'Hi, I'd like to talk to you. Is now a good time?'

Don't be surprised if your animal doesn't want to communicate at the time you've picked. They can decide, and it's important that they do and nothing is forced or coerced. Communication works best when both parties are engaged. Sometimes I'll ask Texas if it's a good time to communicate with him and I'll receive a feeling of 'no' or hear the words 'Not now' and I will respect his decision and try again another time.

The other thing to note is that this step is rarely needed with wild animals. They haven't compromised their natural instincts to fit in with our human lifestyle and tend to jump straight into communicating with us after Step 3.

If you're respectful, that's enough. Communication with wild animals can be short and abrupt, but not always. Keep an open mind about how animal communication works and you'll have more fulfilling and inspirational experiences.

Recap: The five-step method

1. Awaken the breath.
2. Anchor in the heart.
3. Connect heart to heart.
4. 'I love you.'
5. Greeting and intention.

The ritual of disconnection

At the end of a communication, remember your manners. It's rude to just stop. The equivalent would be walking away from a conversation with a human without acknowledging in some way that the conversation has come to an end, perhaps by saying, 'Lovely to see you,' 'Catch up tomorrow,' or 'Thanks for popping in.'

To mark the end of a communication with an animal, I like to thank them and then go through a simple routine of intentionally and visually separating. I do this because it's good to express gratitude to the animal and may encourage them to continue communicating with you, and also because I like to mentally feel that my energy stays with me and their energy stays with them. Even though it is contrary to the belief that we are all energetically linked all of the time, 'like soup in a bowl', what this does is help us move on from difficult, painful or challenging communications with animals. This is especially true for highly emotional communications and when animals have expressed the trauma they've experienced to us. We want to acknowledge them with loving-kindness but not 'take on' their pain and upset. This ritual helps us let go. It doesn't mean we don't care. We care a lot, but we cease to be effective communicators if we allow ourselves to become overwhelmed.

Exercise: The ritual of disconnection

- Silently in your mind, or out loud if you prefer, say to the animal: 'Thank you for communicating with me.'
- Visualize surrounding the animal in a ball of pink light. Have the intention of doing this if you don't find it easy to visualize. The ball is a safe place and pink is a colour of the heart centre.
- Have the intention that you're withdrawing your beam of light, your heart connection with the animal, back into yourself.
- Now visualize, or intend, putting yourself into a ball of pink light.
- Lastly, remind yourself of your connection with the Earth through the soles of your feet on the ground.

Communication guidelines

How to word the questions

Now you've got the method down, you want to think about what you'd like to communicate and, more importantly, how you're going to word the questions. Here are some question guidelines:

- Focus on one question at a time.
- Make it clear and concise.
- Avoid negatives like 'don't', 'can't', 'shouldn't', etc.
- Trust that simple is superior.
- Complicated and complex causes confusion.

Transform your negative into a positive

> *'A single sunbeam is enough to drive away many shadows.'*
> ST FRANCIS OF ASSISI

Only send thoughts of what you do want to happen, rather than what you don't want. If you're concerned about your cat getting run over by a car, you need to transform the negative 'Don't go onto the road or you'll get run over' into something more positive like 'Please stay in the garden where you'll be safe.'

Along the same lines, with a dog, 'You *can't* come with me' transforms into 'Stay here and guard the house' or 'Stay here and have a sleep.' Giving a dog a job often fills them with a sense of purpose and gives them something to do. Remember to thank them when you return.

With a horse, 'You *shouldn't* be trying to break out of your stable' transforms into 'Wait inside until I come and open the door.' Never promise an animal something you can't follow through on. And if they've respected your request, thank them with a healthy treat, brush or butt scratch.

Getting the wording right does matter. Imagine if you were your cat and your human told you, 'Don't scratch the furniture!' with anger in their voice as they bellowed their command at you. You would hear 'Scratch the furniture!' and so would wait until they looked your way then give the deepest, longest scratch you could muster to their prized antique loom armchair, expecting to be rewarded handsomely for your efforts. Instead you would find yourself shouted out, scooped up and bundled out into the cold. What the...?! At the very least you wouldn't be impressed, and most likely, being a cat, you would consider your human the dumbest being on the planet and never trust them again. Mixed messages like these create confusion, erode trust and can be the reason your communication endeavours fail.

Passive hearing and active listening

What I call 'active listening' is vital in animal communication. But what's the difference between 'passive hearing' and 'active listening'?

Passive hearing is when we're partly distracted. It's like listening to the TV at the same time as viewing Facebook subtitles: we're not fully present with either. If we're *passive hearing* it's highly likely we'll lose the connection with the animal and our imagination will start making things up. We can't remain logged on to the animal's unique signature frequency this way.

Active listening is when we give our full attention to the animal we wish to communicate with. Instead of being distracted by thoughts of everything we need to get done or concerns over what's happened or might happen, we're in the present moment with all of our focus on the animal. You don't need to be a Buddhist monk with a zafu to be in the present.

If we're *actively listening*, and I use the word 'listening' loosely here, with the emphasis on 'being receptive', we'll be able to maintain the connection (with practice) and be conscious of the subtlest of impressions expressed by the animal.

It does take concentration, but you'll find that as you practise active listening, it will become easier for you. You can practise it in your daily life too by actively listening to your partner or a friend. Notice how long you can keep focused on one simple task before you find you want to check your Instagram page or refresh your emails. It's become common to flit from this to that nowadays, and many people struggle to concentrate for more than a few minutes. See how you get on and be honest with yourself.

Take responsibility for your emotions

I understand firsthand how we tend to project our own fear out into the world. I used to be scared of dogs. When I was younger, I'd walk down a path, and when dogs came towards me, I'd start to think they could bite me and my fear would build up. Needless to say, the dogs would pick up on my fear and also my thoughts and pictures of them biting me. Very soon they'd have their hackles up and be barking or growling at me. I'd brought about the very thing I'd been scared of. If I'd sent out positive thoughts to the dogs and remained relaxed, as I do now, we could have walked past each other without either of us becoming distressed.

'Keep your teeth in your mouth'

On one occasion I was doing a home visit for a woman who'd requested a consultation because her dog was aggressive. I'd communicated with the dog prior to the visit and explained to him that he'd know it was me and that he was safe because

I would arrive in a red car, I would call his name and I would stand still and tell him, 'It's me, Pea.' I also said to him, 'Please keep your teeth in your mouth and your mouth closed,' and pictured it very clearly. At no point did I communicate, 'Please don't bite me.'

When I pulled up, the woman came outside with her dog, who was barking, growling and spinning around on the end of his lead, highly stressed.

I breathed, relaxed and connected with him. Then, when I got out of my red car, I communicated, 'It's me, Pea. See my red car. You are safe. I love you.' I waited for the recognition whilst I continued slow breathing, relaxing and holding the intention of love. 'Please keep your teeth in your mouth and your mouth closed,' I communicated.

He stopped spinning and barking. I walked in through the gate and up to where he stood with the woman. All the time I was communicating, 'It's me, Pea. You are safe. It's okay to close your mouth.'

He slowly started to relax. He then sniffed me. I continued to communicate, 'You recognize me now? I've been talking to you.' At no point did I hold any fear. I trusted that he would know me. We had communicated and I knew why he was scared.

The woman led me into the house. The dog kept checking me out and I kept reassuring him, 'You are safe. It's me, Pea.'

After about five minutes, I said to the woman, 'You can let him off now.'

She replied, 'It's like he knows you.'

'Yes,' I said.

Once off the lead, the dog lay down and I sat on the floor beside him, giving him slow strokes, reassuring him and letting him know, 'You are safe. I love you.'

Within 10 minutes he rolled over on his side and then surrendered, all paws in the air, inviting tummy strokes.

'I can't believe it,' the woman said. 'He's never done that.'

We continued with our appointment and the reason she'd called me, which was to help with her dog's aggression towards people. I remained on the floor with her dog lying beside me, fully relaxed. By the time I was ready to leave, he'd transformed into his true self – the sweetest dog, who happily walked beside me as I made my way back to my car. He stood at the gate watching me until I was out of sight.

A word or two about fear ... and love

What is fear?

- Fear is the root of all negative emotions.
- Fear is the opposite of love.
- Fear causes tension that in turn blocks energy.

Fear is different from being cautious. We do want to look after our wellbeing, but not hinder our expansion.

What is love?

- Love is the glue or force that holds the universe together.
- Love is acting lovingly.
- Love is the vibration we want to embody and express in animal communication.

The more love we embody, the more powerful we can become.

Communicating with a friend's animal

I feel the most productive way for beginners to learn animal communication is by communicating with the animals of friends or family first. Having your information confirmed by a friend will let you know whether your communication is accurate. Otherwise, how will you learn what feels correct and when you're off? To build awareness of this, practise with verifying questions.

Verifying questions: the what, why and how

What is a verifying question?

A verifying question involves 'what', 'why' and 'how' and can be easily answered by the animal and verified by your friend. It could be, for example, asking your friend's dog, 'What is your favourite food?' You share the response you received from the dog with your friend and they are able to confirm, 'Yes, it *is* the cat's food,' or, 'No, he's actually crazy about raw chicken wings.'

Bear in mind with verifying questions that your friend needs to already know the answer, so you may like to ask them to provide a list for you in advance. These questions are focused on you learning about your animal communication, not giving your friend answers to any concerns they may have about their animal. It would be too much for them to ask this of you when you are starting out and could be detrimental to the wellbeing of the animal as well as a significant blow to your confidence.

Why ask verifying questions?

A verifying question will help you establish the accuracy and truth of what you receive from an animal. These questions will help you discern how your communication is growing. To be able to hone it for accuracy, there needs to be an element of accountability. By the way, when I wrote this sentence, Texas, who was sitting on the desk between the keyboard and me, turned around to face the screen, and I could feel he was approving. He gave me the word 'accountability'. By accountability, Texas and I mean for you to take responsibility for your communication and not presume everything is correct (or incorrect, for that matter). The ethics section at the back of this book (*see page 229*) will also help you to understand the concept of accountability in animal communication.

Without verification, you may struggle to understand and differentiate between when you're receiving information from the animal and when you're not, which is neither helpful to you nor the animal, who may lose interest and even stop communicating altogether. Over time, when you become more skilled, there will be less need for verification, because with (a lot of) practice you'll have learned the difference in resonance between when you're in the flow and receiving information directly from the animal and when it feels 'off' and your mind is making it up. Ah, that meddling mind!

Although you may feel a bit under pressure with verification questions, this is still the best way for you to learn about the nuances of your communication skills.

'*How* do I create verifying questions?'

Here are some more examples that will help you understand the kind of questions you could ask. They can be adapted to suit different species. Notice I'm asking them directly to the animal. You can tweak them, obviously, when you come to asking your friend for verification.

- 'Where do you like to sleep during the day?'
- 'What's your favourite activity?'
- 'Who do you live with?' ('Species?' 'Gender?')
- 'Would you mind letting me know your age?'
- 'Where do you like to sleep at night?'
- 'Who are your friends?'
- 'Where's your favourite walk?'
- 'What's your favourite toy?'
- 'What colour is your rug?'
- 'What do you like to do for fun?'
- 'How do you feel about fireworks?'
- 'Are you allowed to go into your guardian's bedroom?'
- 'How do you feel about the dog walker?'
- 'What do you feel about other cats?'
- 'How do you feel about being picked up?'
- 'Do you enjoy swimming?'
- 'Does anyone share your field?'
- 'How long have you lived with your guardian?'

- 'What do you feel about cars?'
- 'What did you eat for breakfast?'

Ways of receiving the communication

1. Write it down

When receiving the responses from your friend's animal, write them down straight away. This gives your brain something to do; it engages it in activity. Alternatively, you'll need to remember the information, which is hard when you're truly in the flow. You may find that you start to analyse the communication, which gives your brain a chance to give you made-up information. Writing it down makes it less likely that your brain has time to sabotage the communication and you'll get the exact details and wording.

2. Go with your first impressions

Some of the best advice I was given when I was a beginner and am sharing freely now with you is to go with your first impressions. Be present and alert for any slight impression that surfaces and capture it before your mind has time to question it, reject it, discard, censor or manipulate it. Accept the very first thing you receive, however faint or distant. You can even prompt yourself with internal dialogue: *What am I receiving?*

Your first communication with your friend's animal

We'll say you've now talked to a friend who is willing to offer their animal for you to practise communicating with and your friend has provided a list of simple and clear verifying questions. Your friend is aware you are a beginner and has confirmed they know the answer to every verifying question. Be sure to manage their expectations and chose someone who will support your efforts and not belittle or undermine you.

Practice structure: Communicating with a friend's animal

- Preparation (*see Chapter 4*).
- Making a connection (*see Chapter 5*).
- Ask verifying questions and make notes of the answers.
- Ritual of disconnection (*see page 126*).
- Share your communication with your friend and ask them for feedback.

There's strength in vulnerability

> *'Vulnerability is the birthplace of love, belonging, joy, courage, empathy, accountability, and authenticity. It's our most accurate measure of courage.'*
>
> BRENÉ BROWN, RESEARCHER

Animal communication mirrors the school system in a way, because it asks us to share what we've received from an animal in order to verify the answers. This can make us feel vulnerable. Here's the bottom line: there's no way around it. In order to learn how to communicate with animals, you're going to need to reveal what you've received. You have to get familiar with putting yourself on the line. Don't confuse vulnerability with weakness.

Most people struggle with their first attempts; I know I did. It's a fact that you'll never be right all the time. It's an impossibility to be 100 per cent right in intuitive communication. Honest animal communicators will say as much. It's not only intuitive people; scientists often make mistakes (look at NASA's space shuttle experiences), and vets as well as doctors sometimes misdiagnose. So better accept that right now and then let it go. On the positive side, intuition is still *incredibly reliable.*

Professor Marius Usher of Tel Aviv's University School of Psychological Sciences conducted research that forced participants to choose between two options based on gut intuition alone; they made the right call up to 90 per cent of the time. Professor Marius went on to declare, 'Gut instinct can be trusted to make a quality decision.'[1]

With animal communication, everyone struggles at the start, because they're learning to be fluent in an ancient language they've long forgotten. But once you've run your virus test and removed some of those blocks and negative beliefs, you'll be communicating much more quickly, smoothly and easily.

So, my friend, step into your vulnerability, because great strength resides there. Reveal your answers. Receive verification. Put yourself on the line and make it your new norm. As you trust yourself and open up more, your communication will advance and in turn super-charge your confidence.

'How do I know when it's the animal or if I'm making it up?'

- Prepare communication practices that enable you to receive verification.
- When you receive something that is correct, make a note next to it.
- After the communication, look back at how that correct detail came to you and how you felt at the time.
- Question whether you need more time to prepare before starting to communicate and whether you have chosen an appropriate time to communicate.
- Learn to feel the subtle resonance of information: what feels right to you and what feels as though you're making it up. This takes practice and many communications. It will come to you eventually.

- Don't get all het up when you're wrong. The more frustrated you become with yourself, the harder you make it. Remember, it's about the journey, not the destination.

Communicating with animals who have passed over

When connecting with an animal who has passed over, you can use the exact same method as communicating with them when they're still in their physical body. Remember, it's the energetic soul of the animal you're communicating with, not their physical self. If you're communicating with your own animals, you can choose whether to have a photo as a point of focus or recall them in your mind. If you're practising communicating with a friend's animal who has passed over, then you'll be communicating from their photograph.

Why would you want to communicate with animals in spirit?

It can be such a comforting and soul-soothing experience to reconnect with an animal you love after they've passed over. Often there are questions you would like to ask them or things you'd like to let them know. Animals also like to be able to console their humans, answer their questions and release any guilt or trauma they might feel about their passing. The hardest part of death seems to be the belief that it's the end. Final. Yet when we communicate with our animals in their afterlife we find they still exist and are just as loving and devoted as they were when in their body.

How to approach communication with a friend's animal who has passed over

It's an honour to be able to communicate with a friend's animal in spirit if that is what they seek.

Go through some simple verification questions first, so that both of you can be sure that you really are connected to the animal in spirit and that the connection appears strong and accurate. This will enable your friend to trust any information their animal shares that cannot be verified. If the connection is poor or non-existent, make sure you stop and don't continue. Rest, reset and try again another day.

As a beginner, make sure you're not entering into anything highly emotive or that will put you in an impossible position. For instance, you may wish to leave to an experienced professional questions like 'Did I let them down?' or 'If I had done it differently, would they still be alive?' I understand why people ask these questions, but as an animal communicator, they put you under so much pressure, and if the animal doesn't give the answer the guardian is hoping for, as their friend, you could find yourself in a very tricky situation. So leave these emotive questions to a professional who is equipped to handle them and who is not connected to your friend.

Recognizing your way of communicating

Once you've started to communicate with animals, set some time aside to think about your communication. In Chapter 3 we looked at the different methods of sending and receiving information with animals. After you've completed a communication, look at how you received information and how you sent information.

Receiving

- Were you mostly correct when receiving picture images?
- Or were emotions the strongest and more reliable method?
- Perhaps, like me, you found that words came to you before anything else?
- Could you feel sensations in your body as the animal replied to you?
- Were you able to taste the flavour of their favourite food and feel the texture of it?
- Could you smell it?
- Did you have a gut instinct and 'just knew' what the animal was expressing?

Sending

- Did you find it easy to send a picture to the animal or were you relying solely on words as thought forms to describe what you meant?
- Did you manage to share an emotion as you asked an emotional question?

It will be helpful for you to become familiar with your own communication style. By understanding what happens behind the scenes, you'll become more in tune with what happens on the stage, so to speak. You'll discover what's working and the way it works, and when you continue to practise over many months, you can focus on honing the areas needing improvement. I'll help with this in Part III.

Your first communication with your own animal

By now, you've practised with your friend's animal. You've looked at your communication style. Now you want to have an exchange with your own animal.

Practice structure: Communicating with your own animal

- Preparation (*see Chapter 4*).
- Making a connection (*see Chapter 5*).
- Ask opening questions and make notes of the answers (*see opposite*).

- Ritual of disconnection (*see page 126*).
- Reward your animal with affection, play time, a great hack or delicious treat and thank them for helping you learn to communicate with them. This will encourage them to engage another time and we all like to be thanked.

Opening questions

It's really nice to start your first communications with your animal with some positive and encouraging questions that they will enjoy answering. While these can't necessarily be verified, they are useful as a means to engage your animal and to get the communication flowing. Here are a few examples:

- 'How are you feeling today?'
- 'What are you most enjoying today?'
- 'Where do you like to spend time?'
- 'What do you love about your life?'
- 'What brings you most joy?'

Do avoid entering into areas of concern like physical problems, behaviour you find strange or unacceptable, or discussing anything like their past, which may be upsetting or hard for them to express, or for that matter for you to receive at this early stage. It really is better for both of you to start off lightly and to make it fun and rewarding for you both.

A little note: most people find it much harder to communicate with their own animals. But relax, I've got you covered. I've dedicated the whole of the next chapter to helping you with it.

Woo-hoo!

You've now started communicating with animals. It's time for a happy dance. Yes, go for it! Don't hold back! There's nothing like dancing to raise your vibration. Adding joy and acknowledgement into your communication journey will help shift your vibration from one of doubt or disbelief into 'Oh yeah, I'm doing it, baby!'

Life just got a whole lot more exciting!

SUMMARY

- The Heart-to-Heart method includes five steps that guide you into a connection with an animal.
- It's good to have manners with animals.
- The ritual of disconnection is a clean and protective technique to end a communication.
- Verifying questions help you learn your communication style, develop clarity and improve accuracy.

- Active listening is the key to retaining focus and connection.
- There are two basic ways to approach communicating with animals: face to face or through photographs.
- Use the same five-step method to connect with an animal in spirit as you do an animal in body.
- Great strength lies in vulnerability.

Chapter 6

Effective Steps to Communicating with Your Own Animals

'Knowing yourself is the beginning of all wisdom.'

ARISTOTLE, PHILOSOPHER

You may be surprised to learn that this chapter turns the spotlight on you. If you see yourself down stage centre (or DSC, as I used to say in the theatre biz) with a huge follow-spot on you, then you'll be cheering. However, if the idea of being in the spotlight has you running for the wings, don't worry, I totally understand.

This chapter benefits you and your alter ego. The reason why? Because as soon as we start to communicate with animals, everything that stops us creating a connection with them will be flagged up so that it can be seen clearly, worked with and then ultimately released.

When I started out, I soon learned that I had blocks to dissolve before I could progress. These blocks prevented me from being a clear channel to send or receive information. When I went into denial over any of these blocks, Morgan would bring my focus to them, sometimes in a dramatic way.

On one of my particular issues, I failed to react to his gentle nudges for a while, so in the end he gave me a 'hard shove' to get my attention. The primary issue I didn't want to face was how I felt about myself. I'd had a childhood that had failed to meet my emotional needs (it's not surprising I turned to animals for their unconditional love) and I was painfully shy, which brought its own dilemmas. Morgan wanted me to let go of this old image of myself; he wanted me to realize I was different now and that I was just hanging on to a story that was holding me back. He encouraged me to step into my power and acknowledge my self-worth, and he did this by risking his own life. Thankfully I engaged with the block I was so stuck on, despite it being a difficult one, and Morgan survived. In hindsight, that shift was the second greatest gift he ever gave me. The first was when he introduced me to animal communication.

I don't want your animals to go to such extreme lengths to help you work through anything that hinders your ability to communicate with them, so I've devised valuable tools and techniques to help you over the bumps, round the humps and to unstick wherever you might feel stuck. You might feel they don't all apply to you, and that's okay. Find the ones that do (if any) and practise them. Engaging with the obstacles as they arise is an essential part of your journey. They are gifts for you to give time to, reflect on and then transform. Every challenge can be viewed as a stepping stone on your path of growing intuition and awakening.

'Why is it harder to communicate with my own animals?'

You might be thinking, *Surely it's easier to communicate with an animal I know well and love.* I agree that would make sense, but *only* once you really trust your communication. When you're starting out, it seems quite a struggle to trust it's them sending information and not yourself making it all up, because you feel you already understand them. As I've already shared, the best starting point for learning animal communication is through communicating with the animals of your friends or family and receiving validation through verifying questions. This approach then leads to communicating with your own animal(s) to understand their thoughts and feelings on life, love and the universe.

Motivate your mojo

Your mental processes and emotional clarity will either hinder or enhance your animal communication. If you recognize that you find it hard to trust, or experience self-doubt or low self-esteem, you might like to explore the following ways to boost your mojo.

Right at the outset, understand that in no way is this a judgement on how you think or feel. We're all at different places, depending on our life experiences and ability to adjust, self-regulate and commit to our self-care and growth. Use the information in this chapter as helpful guidelines and engage with what resonates with you personally.

Let me ease you in gently by first looking at good communication practice.

Good practice model for receiving intuitive information

- *Keep it light:* Be as light-hearted as possible.
- *Smile softly:* Your energy will change and become more open.
- *Be playful:* The more fun you make it, the easier it will be for you as well as more enjoyable for the animal.
- *Stop trying so hard:* Resist the need to be perfect or correct. Have you noticed when you really want something it can be difficult to achieve?
- *Pick your moment:* See when works best for you, your energy level and the animal. (I've found I prefer to communicate in the morning.)

- *Let go of logic:* Logic cramps your intuition, so be willing to really see and listen and enter into a relationship with animals that goes beyond the concepts of what you feel you know.
- *Craving instant results:* Slow down, what's the rush? If you feel desperate, you'll receive the opposite of what you're hoping for. Enjoy learning and growing, there is no final destination in animal communication.
- *Don't edit:* Go with everything and anything, however quirky it seems. If you change something you receive to what you 'think' it might mean, you can turn a correct impression into a nonsensical one.
- *Note everything down:* It will occupy the logical, analytical side of your mind, giving it less opportunity to sabotage what you receive, and it means you can stay in the flow, because you won't need to focus on remembering the details.
- *Own your power:* Stop invalidating your own potential to communicate with animals. Your animals can become frustrated when you continue to dismiss an understanding of their thoughts and feelings.
- *Take a leap of faith:* At some point, to hone your ability, you'll have to take a leap of faith and just go for it, without worrying about failure, or what your folks will say. Just immerse yourself heart and soul. Suspend your beliefs and be willing to relinquish absolutes and certainty.

Three techniques to unlock blocks

These three techniques guide you in how to approach the opening communications with your animals to take the pressure off and to gain your animal's interest in the topic of conversation.

1. Ask the animal for help

You can say to your animal, 'Please help me communicate with you, I'm just a beginner and I know you're really good at this.' You can also ask them to be patient: 'Please be patient with me as I learn to trust myself and trust that I can communicate with you.'

2. Ask the animal for advice

Who doesn't like being asked for advice? Animals love to be asked. It's so rare that a human even considers that their animal may have the answer to their dilemma.

Sometimes people find it very hard to talk to another human, but they'll talk to their dog, horse or rabbit. Why is that? Because humans are often tired of the human race and the way the species is so judging? Perhaps this is also why humans find it hard to trust each other?

Advice suggestions:

- *Relationship stuff:* Ask your animal if they like your new partner. What do they feel about them? How might you bring more joy to your relationship?

- *Changing job:* If you're thinking of following your passion and applying for your dream job, ask if they have a comment about this. Would it be for your highest good to change your career?
- *Moving home:* If you're thinking of moving house, ask them to comment on this. Ask them where they think would be good for you to live. If you have a choice between two locations, which would they prefer?

3. Ask the animal for their opinion

In workshops, I have found animals to be very patient teachers and I have witnessed people's barriers coming down as soon as an animal enters the room. Just walks into the room – that's how powerful animals are. They seem to have a disarming ability to reach right into people's hearts. When they are around, people soften, open and smile. No wonder we ask animals to work in therapy settings – where children will only read to dogs, where horses will mirror adult issues needing transformation, or cats will purr into human hearts and prevent loneliness.

Animals bring out the best in people and are the gateway to a higher awareness. They also have a lot to say and will offer opinions on matters if you take the time to ask them. There is nothing you can't discuss with your animals.

You could ask them about:

- their favourite walk
- what they feel about the new vet
- even what they feel about global warming or human greed

The only limitation is your own imagination and whether or not your animal wants to follow your line of enquiry. They may find it boring! Always respect their free will.

Ten ways to recognize when communication has occurred

I've had dogs as guest teachers at my workshops and when we've asked the question, 'Who's your best friend?', they have crossed the room and put their paws on their guardian's lap or sat and looked up into their face, obviously communicating to everyone in the room: 'They are!' One dog even climbed onto his guardian's lap – and he'd never done that before. The man, despite being very sceptical at the beginning (he had been 'volunteered' by his wife, who was attending), accepted his dog's answer because of his visual demonstration of it.

Here are 10 signs that will help you understand that you've been able to communicate with your best friend:

1. You'll feel it in your body.
2. You'll respond emotionally.
3. You'll taste or smell things that weren't part of your experience before you began communicating.
4. Your animal will try to 'show' you the answer to a question.
5. Your animal will be different with you.
6. They may be more attentive.
7. Their behaviour will change.
8. They'll be more affectionate, more peaceful or calm.
9. They'll look at you differently, because they know that you know them.
10. You'll become even closer.

When Morgan had just arrived and was very sad, Texas was very wary of him and liked to keep his distance. I communicated with Morgan and he shared why he was sad. And from that moment, he was able to let go of his past and commit fully to his new family. It was obvious communication had taken place and had been effective, because the change in Texas was instant: he visibly relaxed and accepted Morgan's presence.

Three ways to get out of your own way

Your ability to examine yourself and adjust is the key for success in living life with greater compassion and kindness in all of your inter-species relationships. These three stages will provide you with the tools to start self-regulation, regardless of your inclinations, past experiences or personality traits.

1. The belief process

Communicate with your animal as though they can understand you. You can make it an experiment or even better a fun game between you and your friend.

Exercise: The belief process

- Over the next four weeks, believe that your animal understands everything you communicate through your verbal words or thoughts.
- Make notes of any changes in the way they relate to you.
- Make notes of anything you receive.
- At the end of the process, reflect on the changes you observe in your animal and their relationship with you.

I'd love you to share your experiences on my Facebook page (*see page 243*) as accountability for yourself and encouragement to others.

2. The peaceful mind

Another barrier to communicating with an animal, especially our own, is our thoughts. The HeartMath Institute states that peace of mind brings a rhythmic balance to both brain and heart waves, which they call 'coherence'. This coherence can have a profound effect on an animal.

Make a point of monitoring your thoughts prior to communicating and take responsibility to bring your mind into a peaceful state. A simple method of doing this is to breathe in to the word 'peaceful' and breathe out to 'mind'. I prefer to do it with my eyes closed.

3. The soft heart

Extensive research by the HeartMath Institute has revealed that the heart's magnetic field radiates outside the body and can affect other people as well as animals.[1] It carries transmissions of information, data if you like, between species, which can be accessed by intuition.

The research also explored the electrophysiology of intuition and showed that human emotions could reach non-human animals.[2] Some emotions are beneficial of course, such as when you're feeling calm and loving towards your animal. However, if you've had a stressful day, make sure you release the stress before you start animal communication, perhaps by having a hot bath, going for a jog, or trying the following exercise.

Exercise: The heart-softening technique

This technique can help activate the para-sympathetic nervous system and relieve stress, bringing a feeling of peace and a greater heart connection. It will also bring a lightness and softness to your heart.

Preparation

- Before you begin, take a moment to observe how you're feeling.
- Take a deep breath in and slow breath out to mark the beginning of your practice.

Technique

- Place one hand on your heart and the other hand, palm towards you, just in front of your mouth.
- Breathe in through your nose, following the airflow down to your heart.
- Breathe out through your mouth, following the airflow up to your mouth and breathing out as if you're blowing out a candle. Notice the feeling of your breath on your palm.
- Repeat, making your breath lighter and lighter, softer and softer, until you can barely perceive it on your palm when you breathe out.
- Continue for three to four minutes with the intention of making your breath softer and softer.

Observation

- Relax your hands, open your eyes and observe how you feel now.
- How does it compare to before you began the technique?

- How does your heart feel now?

Through intentionally linking your breathing with your heart awareness, you'll find that by softening your breath, you will also soften your heart.

Catch a limiting belief and let it go

> *'I have no special talent. I am passionately curious.'*
> ALBERT EINSTEIN, THEORETICAL PHYSICIST

We have to be careful of limiting beliefs that decree what *is* and *is not* possible. What we know is changing all the time. The BBC *Blue Planet 2* series revealed, 'Many scientists now believe life on Earth may have begun around a hydro-volcanic vent 4 billion years ago. We now know these vents hold as much life as a tropical rainforest with half a million individual animals per square metre.'[3] *Blue Planet* also revealed that we're now aware that the moons of Jupiter and Saturn have deep seas and that much of Earth's volcanic activity occurs in the deep.

With new discoveries being made all the time, being open-minded and curious serves us better than remaining closed and stuck. By failing to consider new possibilities, we're missing out on so much. So, can a cat communicate to you from behind a piano? You bet she can. Can you hear her? As long as your consciousness refuses to embrace the possibility, it will remain beyond your experience. If you believe you can, you've got a much stronger chance.

Self-regulation

There is a Cherokee legend called 'Two Wolves'.[4] It goes like this:

An old Cherokee is teaching his grandson about life.

'A fight is going on inside me,' he says to the boy. 'It's a terrible fight and it is between two wolves. One is evil – he is anger, envy, sorrow, regret, greed, arrogance, self-pity, guilt, resentment, inferiority, lies, false pride, superiority and ego.

'The other is good – he is joy, peace, love, hope, serenity, humility, kindness, benevolence, empathy, generosity, truth, compassion and faith. The same fight is going on inside you – and inside every other person too.'

The grandson thinks about it for a minute and then asks, 'Which wolf will win?'

The old Cherokee simply replies, 'The one you feed.'

We all have some light and dark to our personality. My black dog friend, Bodhi, taught me to engage with my shadow side rather than ignore it. Bodhi reminded me that wherever I went, my shadow followed me, so it was better to make it a friend rather than deny it existed. He asked me to be conscious of when my shadow self was jeopardizing my progress. I've found the more I recognize that part of myself, the better I am at embodying love and compassion. I observe myself, reflect and self-regulate as often as I can.

Observing ourselves, reflecting and self-regulating can be divided up into four areas:

1. *Physical:* Physical flexibility, endurance and strength.
2. *Emotional:* Emotional flexibility, a positive outlook and supportive relationships.
3. *Mental:* Mental flexibility, focus and the ability to integrate multiple points of view.
4. *Spiritual:* Commitment to core values, intuition and tolerance of others' values and beliefs.

If you feel you're struggling with any aspect of communicating with your animals, take a look at these four areas and be honest about whether you need to give some time and energy to furthering a particular aspect of yourself. You'll have a feeling of the area where you may be stuck or less flexible. For instance, perhaps you can recognize that you are quick to dismiss other people's points of view. This could indicate your mental flexibility needs some help. If you struggle to view things with a positive outlook, perhaps your emotional core needs strengthening or you need to cultivate more positive relationships in your life to support you. There are many classes and courses that tailor to each of these areas and it's down to you to do some research and see what interests you and will bring you joy. Focus on enhancing one area at a time over a number of weeks or months and see how that brings you into greater balance and enhances your animal communication skills.

I tend to fall down on the physical area, as I sit down a lot of the day, so having Grace, the new dog in my life, and getting out to walk her every day helps me a great deal.

Let's talk about trust

'Trust yourself, then you will know how to live.'
Johann Wolfgang von Goethe, writer and statesman

I really want to focus more on trust in this chapter, because how you trust in your everyday life, or not, will massively impact on your ability to trust your animal communication.

In workshops, I mention growth, the comfort zone and energy, and I want to share these with you too. When you trust yourself, it's much easier to take the risks needed to live an expansive life. Trust is your doorway to transformation as well as meaningful communication with animals. The following pointers will help you understand where you stand on the trust scale.

1. Your personal growth needs risk

Muhammad Ali said, 'He who is not courageous enough to take risks will accomplish nothing in life.' With trust, you can take on something new or do things that you might find difficult or challenging. You may feel some fear, but you are filled with courage. Taking risks will enhance your personal growth. If there is something you've always wanted to do, I encourage you to do it. Whether it's swimming in the ocean with wild dolphins or taking a long-haul flight by yourself to kayak with killer whales, think of something you want to do but find challenging and summon up the courage to give it a go.

2. Skip over the edge of your comfort zone

We all know what the comfort zone is, but how many of us are brave enough to step outside it? What do we think will happen if we skip over the perimeter? If we stay where we are, we have the same old, dull, boring, repetitive, yawn, yawn life. Even the comfort zone can become as exciting as an old sock.

A comfort zone in animal communication is a self-limiting restriction that will inhibit your communication and the deep and moving details animals could share with you. All you've got to do is step over the edge.

3. Trust energizes your life

Living a life with trust enables you to embody more energy. Why? Because instead of wasting it worrying about what happened in the past or what could happen in the future, you have the belief that whatever is happening right now is happening for a reason and everything will work out okay. You'll become aligned with universal life-force energy and be able to emit this feeling of harmony out into the world. Living in alignment will then enable you to engage with the mystery of life. And this is a powerful place to be.

The mantra 'I trust'

A mantra is a frequently repeated statement. This 'I trust' mantra (*below*) can help reprogram limiting mental patterning. You might like to record this and then play it back when you can lie down with eyes closed and completely surrender to the words. Try repeating each sentence. During the day you might prefer to repeat a sentence out loud. You could sing it or shout it from a mountaintop. You could write it down on a sticky note and attach it to your laptop, the dash of your car, your fridge door or bathroom mirror. See what works for you. Be creative.

I trust

I trust.

I trust in myself.

I trust in my love of animals.

I trust I can be relaxed and calm.

I trust I have this ability.

I trust I am strong.

I trust that my mind is open.

I trust worries are released.

I trust I have energy.

I trust I have positive thoughts.

I trust in life.

I trust everything I need is within me.

I trust everything I need I already have.

I trust in my journey.

I trust in my ability to transform obstacles into opportunities for growth.

I trust in loving relationships.

I trust offers of support.

I trust I am able to attract healing relationships.

I trust in my life purpose.

I trust my life purpose will be fulfilled.

I trust in divine timing and release all desire of achievement right now.

I trust anything that no longer serves me will make space for something new.

I trust in my love.

I trust in my compassion.

I trust myself.

I trust.

Raise your vibes

> *'Appreciating what shows up in your life changes your personal vibration. Gratitude elevates your life to a higher frequency.'*
> OPRAH WINFREY, MEDIA PROPRIETOR

By now you're aware that how you feel about yourself can impact on your animal communication ability. So this is not just about listening to animals, it's about listening to yourself. As you progress in your communication with animals, you will face internal barriers. But with these exercises, approaches and meditations, you have the tools in your toolkit to unlock any blocks, take on trust and power up your potential.

You are your own guru.

You know yourself better than anyone – well, except your animals, who know you better than you do!

Here are two exercises to raise your vibes:

Exercise: My gratitude practice

This helps enhance gratitude and refocuses you on joyfulness and appreciation. This shift also creates chemicals of wellbeing, leading to less stress, improved health and a much more positive outlook on life.

It's simple. Just list 10–20 things you are grateful for.

Here are some of mine to start you off:

- Animal companions
- My partner
- A hairdryer
- Pink roses
- Turquoise seas
- Wild dolphins
- Good coffee
- A warm house
- Great friends
- Reading
- Travel abroad

Exercise: Self-compassion cultivation

Self-compassion is so beneficial. How can we expect ourselves to be compassionate to other species, especially when they're doing something we find frustrating, if we're not able to show that same level of love towards ourselves?

- Write the letter 'I' on a sheet of printing paper. 'I' signifies you: all your talents, achievements, everything you're capable of, your physical and mental qualities, and your emotional ones too.
- Then start to write down positive aspects about yourself. Then keep adding to them. For examples: 'Enjoy travelling.' 'Aim to be patient.' 'Scoop the poop.' 'Cook for my partner.'

- When you review your 'I' declarations, you might find that you're doing pretty well, actually, and that there aren't so many things to work on as you thought. Focus on your positives. Give yourself a break. Be kind. Be compassionate. If not you, then who?

Let me hear your body talk

I've shared a lot about how our emotions and thoughts affect our ability to communicate well. To end this chapter I also want to share a physical technique with you. It opens up your pectoral area, allowing space for your heart to open like a lotus flower, and realigns the spinal column, which improves respiration and circulation.

Exercise: Standing starfish pose (the five-minute miracle)

The benefits of the standing starfish pose are that it lengthens, opens and energizes the whole body. Confidence will beam out of your belly and spine, down your arms and into your fingertips. It only takes five minutes, but you'll be surprised how it can change how you feel. This is also a great one to do before you communicate with your animals.

- Begin standing with your feet together and your arms by your side, fingers pointing to the ground. Have your feet wide apart, facing forward and parallel. Contract your naval and lengthen your spine towards the sky. Breathe and stabilize.

- Breathing in, lift your arms into a 'T' shape, palms facing the ground. Check your feet are under your wrists. Press your weight into your feet, rooting them into the Earth.
- Continue to lengthen your spine towards the sky while squeezing your sitting bones together to pull your tailbone down towards the Earth.
- Extend your arms and fingertips to the sides and relax your shoulders back and down, gently opening your chest.
- Feel your body expanding out in five directions, like a starfish.
- Hold the starfish pose for three to six long, slow breaths.
- To release it, bring your feet back together and that's it!

You did it!

> *'All our dreams can come true when we have the courage to pursue them.'*
> Walt Disney, entrepreneur

Your mind has now been expanded by these new experiences and can't return to old dimensions. You can't undo knowledge. There's no turning back. You've already increased your awareness and raised your consciousness.

SUMMARY

- The good practice model is beneficial for effective communication with animals.
- Dissolve inner blocks by taking the pressure off yourself and asking for the animal's advice.
- Acknowledge when communication has occurred and give yourself a high-five.
- Listen to your 'good wolf' and feed that one.
- Trust is your doorway to transformation and meaningful communication with animals.

Part III

DEVELOPING YOUR COMMUNICATION WITH ANIMALS

'Be infinitely flexible and constantly amazed.'

JASON KRAVITS, ACTOR

Chapter 7

Troubleshooting for Beginners

'Success always demands a greater effort.'

WINSTON CHURCHILL, FORMER BRITISH PRIME MINISTER

If you've got past the last chapter and are still with me, I know you're keen! Getting this far means you really want to do this, you're not giving up and making a difference to animals' wellbeing is important to you. I'm chuffed to bits. Join the club. You're an animal ambassador.

In this chapter I really want to explore the problems and challenges that can seem like insurmountable boulders. With a few tweaks, you can turn those huge boulders into stepping stones to growth and success. I'll address the most common challenges people experience and offer a handful of techniques you can work on to transform them. Practise the ones that connect with you.

The three 'P's

The three 'P's I'm talking about here are *practice*, *patience* and *persistence*. We're going to be looking at these and why you need to make them your best friends. We'll also be looking at practice approaches. Are you sitting comfortably? Then we'll begin.

When it comes to communicating with animals, there's no difference between your own natural abilities and mine. I remember my own teacher said this when I was a beginner. What sets people who have become skilled at animal communication apart from the rest is years of practice, fathoms of patience and the persistence of a salmon. To put it succinctly: determination. Animal communication meant too much to us to give up.

1. Practice

The key to building the telepathic muscle is practice, practice and more practice – just like building any muscle or learning anything well. You wouldn't expect to communicate fluently in Italian after one class in that language. Neither can you expect automatic success after a handful of attempts to communicate with animals. Occasionally I witness individuals feeling very disappointed, even angry or frustrated, when they're not perfect on their very first attempts. Humans – they baffle me more than any other species. Why do people create such incredible expectations of themselves?

I suggest if you get one single piece of detail correct in your early attempts at animal communication, you give thanks and throw a party! It's a cause for celebration and a sign you're heading in the right direction. In basic dog training we're taught to ignore what we consider wrong behaviour (unless it's going to be hurtful or dangerous) and to praise the dog every time they're doing something we consider right. Dogs learn more quickly this way. I invite you to take the same approach with yourself. You can even have a dog treat if you really want one!

When you're starting out, I suggest you practise communicating with an animal once a week. I'm suggesting once a week because most people have hectic lives and I think this commitment is doable. If you're freaking out at the thought of a weekly practice, make it fortnightly or monthly. What's important is that you keep to your commitment and communicate regularly.

2. Patience

We can all be impatient when we're trying to learn something new. Do you remember when you first started to learn how to drive? All you really wanted to do was to drive to the beach, not go through 'forward, reverse, mirror, signal, manoeuvre', step by step, week after week. Yet now it feels like second nature, right? It also takes patience to master all the different elements of basic animal communication. It can be frustrating at times, sure, but the outcome is incredible.

3. Persistence

Persistence is the continuation in a course of action *in spite of* difficulty or opposition. It's about being determined, resolute, purposeful and steadfast. Ask any successful person who started from humble beginnings how they did it and they'll tell you they didn't give up. Despite setbacks, despite people dismissing their ideas, they continued on because they felt passionate about what they were doing and had a belief it would work. If you adopt this 'P' as part of your toolkit, your success is guaranteed.

The ABC of animal communication

> *'Attitude is a little thing that makes a BIG difference.'*
>
> WINSTON CHURCHILL, FORMER BRITISH PRIME MINISTER

Many of the solutions to difficulties with animal communication can be summarized in this ABC, making these reliable points to return to whenever you feel a bit lost.

A: Adjust your attitude

Your attitude towards animals will influence how receptive you are to what they're communicating and how willing they are to communicate with you. A condescending attitude that animals are less bright, less evolved and lower in the scheme of things will hinder a heart-led connection. Communication with non-human animals, or humans for that matter, is much more successful when the other being is treated with respect and as a potential teacher. This attitude will allow them to express themselves openly and honestly to you without diminishing their intelligence, wisdom and knowledge. In time it could even elevate and expand your relationship.

B: Beware biology

The biological traits of an animal are fascinating, but they can also be limiting. If you put an animal into a box based on scientific proof and conventional views of who they are as a species, you can also restrict the possibilities of seeing them clearly as a whole and spiritual individual encased in a physical vessel.

There was a lovely learning experience for students attending my workshop training in Australia in 2016. We were blessed with a horse, numerous breeds and ages of dogs, even chickens, a parrot, a cat and a snake. But the animal who made the biggest impression and had people queuing up in their tea break to meet him was our guest teacher, Trevor – a charismatic, opinionated and wise being in the body of a guinea pig.

C: Cultivate compassion

The definition of 'compassion' is 'to show kindness, caring and a willingness to help others'. When you have compassion, you're putting yourself into someone else's shoes (or paws) and really feeling for them. A simple way to nurture these qualities is by refocusing your efforts into embodying softness. Soften your emotions, soften your thoughts and soften your intentions.

Five common challenges in animal communication

> *'Difficulties are the things that show what we are.'*
> EPICTETUS, PHILOSOPHER

When I feel blocked, I choose to see it as another useful learning step in my growth and development, rather than letting it scare me into submission or discourage me so much that I stop communicating altogether. In my view, a roadblock is just another prompt to find a new route that might even lead to stunning views. I hope you can learn to see them as signs on your journey too.

So, what are the most common blocks and how do you get past them?

1. Being physically ungrounded

Animal communication is an earthy, grounded, solid type of work, contrary to the airy-fairy label proffered by those who haven't experienced it. Animals are grounded and require us to be too.

Solution: Embody your body

To be effective, make sure you are *in* your body. A good level of care for your body will support your animal communication. You won't have to become a yoga ninja – simply empower your body with regular exercise, nutritious food, plenty of water, time in nature and plenty of relaxation and rest.

2. Feeling fearful of failure or getting it wrong

This is the most common block. Everyone wants to be accurate. Fear can cause anyone to freeze so that receiving anything from an animal can become impossible.

Solution: Express neutrality

The remedy for fear of failure or getting it wrong is to adopt a neutral mindset instead. Neutrality is helpful with so many elements of animal communication, but especially when we lose our sense of calm or start putting ourselves under pressure to be perfect. In the heart-to-heart connection with an animal, there is no fear because there is no want, no need and no desire.

3. Pushing too hard

You want to make a difference to animals and you want to do it with integrity. That's fine, but if you push too hard, your desire starts to get in the way. Authentic animal communication is easy and flowing.

Solution: Breathe

A powerful way to stop pushing or trying so hard is through breathing. Through conscious and focused breathing you can bring yourself to the present moment, let go of mental 'monkey chatter', relax your body and relax your mind. Breathing in this way will also open your chest and heart area and bring your awareness back to love and being. Whales and dolphins are excellent conscious breathers. They rely on it for their survival. Try and be more whale or dolphin-like and you'll soon shift from pushing into composure.

4. Attachment

Having an attachment to the outcome of a communication will only get you in a tangle and overly anxious. It will be more than likely that your mental projections will prevent the animal's true communication from reaching you. You'll be coming from ego rather than your heart.

Solution: Listen with your heart

From very early on we're encouraged to navigate life from our intellect rather than our gut feelings and intuition. When communicating with animals, you'll need to turn this around and focus on your feelings. People who have professions in which they're recognized and rewarded for their mental ability often struggle to move out of this familiar head-centred comfort zone down into the heart area of emotion, intuition and just knowing: the great unknown. Yet it's crucial for reawakening our telepathic abilities with animals. I encourage you to listen with your heart.

5. Tired, angry, panicked or stressed

All of these aspects are barriers to clear and effective communication. Instead of powering on, learn to step back, take time out and reset yourself.

Solution: Let the animals teach you

One of the most beautiful and rewarding elements of animal communication is when we allow the animals to teach us. Animals can teach us how to be playful and how to love. They can teach us to be friendly and forgiving. They can also teach us to be quiet and still – perfect pointers for communication. When animals are tired, they sleep. When they're angry, they struggle to learn. When they're panicked, they can't listen clearly. When they're stressed, they can be reactive. They communicate best when they're open and calm. This is another lesson we can learn from them.

You can grow your skills

'In a gentle way, you can shake the world.'

MAHATMA GANDHI, ACTIVIST

Whenever you encounter a new type of challenge, it's always a chance to develop a new set of skills. Whatever the challenge is, I ask you to accept it and engage with it. By noting your blocks, filters and misperceptions, you can begin to overcome them.

- Name the challenge out loud. It will diminish some of the power you give it.
- Engage with it rather than trying to make it disappear – it won't.
- Adopt it as your teacher rather than a pest.
- Ask what you have to learn here.
- Don't fight it – be compassionate and treat it like a friend.
- Ask yourself, are you focused on developing your skills or in denial?
- Take responsibility; laziness gets you nowhere fast.
- Remember, you have to put the effort in to reap the rewards.

Release tension

Many of us are aware that we hold the tension of unresolved feelings in our body. One simple way to start releasing them is through a physical movement called the 'cat stretch', which can help to release muscle tension in the shoulders, neck and spine. It helps to bring us back into a calm state of awareness and it's a nice exercise to do before you begin a communication.

Exercise: Cat stretch tension release

Note: Talk to your doctor before doing this if you have a back condition or injury or problems with your wrists.

- *Start on your hands and knees.* Use a rug or yoga mat. Create a 'table top' position with your wrists directly underneath your shoulders and your knees directly underneath your hips. Make your back flat and neutral. Create a straight line from your head to your tailbone and lower your gaze.
- *Spread your fingers* with your middle finger facing forwards and press your fingertips into the ground.
- *Connect with your breath.* Inhale deeply through your nose, pause, then slowly exhale through your gently parted lips. Inhale again.
- *Exhale and round your back* and draw your naval towards your spine. Tuck your tailbone under and lower your chin to your chest, rounding your spine into a 'C'-shape or angry cat pose. Breathe in and out three times.
- *Inhale and reverse.* Slowly release your naval and return to the neutral flat back position. Still inhaling, lift your chest and look up. Keep your arms strong and shoulder blades back and down.

- *Repeat the entire movement* (points four and five) a few times. I choose eight times.

Exercise: The surrender roll down

- As an alternative, you can do a roll down:
- Stand with your feet hip-width apart, hands relaxed down by your thighs.
- Slowly roll your body down as you breathe out, allowing your hands to glide down your legs to control the movement. Soften your knees a little and draw up your naval to support your back.
- Go as far as is comfortable and take a few breaths, surrender, waggle dance your arms and allow tension to leave you.
- Return by rolling slowly back up to standing as you breathe in.

Dissolve the barriers to love

> *'Seek and find all the barriers within yourself that you have built against love.'*
>
> RUMI, POET

As we've already mentioned, when we struggle to receive communication from an animal, it can be because our heart is closed, shielded or shut down. Perhaps our feelings have been hurt by another person, the death of an animal or unresolved guilt or grief. For whatever reason, barriers have gone up around our heart in order to protect it, and these can cause animal communication to be severely limited.

Dissolving the barriers to love starts with loving yourself. That way, you can start to gently dissolve them until they disappear altogether.

Exercise: Dissolving the barriers to love

Step 1: Your body

Start with your body. Acknowledge what you feel about your body, without trying to change your feelings. This is a body honouring, not a body shaming based on body shape.

- Have a 'conscious' bath once a fortnight, gifting yourself undistracted time to feel what it's like to be in your body.
- Care for your body with a massage.
- Nurture your body with some exercise.
- Scan your body regularly to bring more body awareness.

Step 2: Your mind

Have you ever considered how you speak to yourself? Are you accepting, compassionate and loving? Or are your words and thoughts critical?

- Observe how your negative talk feels in your body, then say something positive to yourself and notice the difference.
- Go further by noticing if what you're saying sounds like someone else, perhaps your mum or dad, a teacher or partner.
- Learn to recognize when you're being unkind to yourself.

Step 3: Your heart

When was the last time you took time just to be with your heart?

- Observe in this moment, as you breathe, do you feel your heart is open or closed?
- Is it feeling light and expansive or heavy and restricted?
- Trust whatever you sense as your truth.
- If you find yourself blocking or distrusting it, accept this as a spotlight on a barrier you have towards trusting and loving yourself.

Inner child writing

> *'Caring for your inner child has a powerful and surprisingly quick result: Do it and the child heals.'*
> Martha Beck, sociologist

Acknowledging and interacting with your inner child is an extremely powerful way to get to the core of deep issues. There are a number of methods, but this is my favourite, and I've used it many times to resolve my confusion.

Exercise: Inner child writing

Before you begin, find a place where you'll be uninterrupted, comfortable and feel safe to be vulnerable. You'll need a notepad and pen and might like to wrap yourself up in a blanket.

- *Write the question with your dominant (writing) hand.* Begin with 'Dear [your name]' and continue with any question you're struggling with that relates to yourself, for example: 'Dear [Name], Why am I struggling to be calm and present?' 'Dear [Name], Why can't I receive my animal's communication?'
- *Write the answer with your non-dominant hand.* Write the first thought that comes into your head. Don't worry about it being a scribble or scrawl. This is your inner child speaking now and they don't care how it looks.
- *Continue questioning* with your dominant hand and answering with your non-dominant hand until you find insight or recognize the truth of the issue.
- *Thank your inner child.* Promise to listen to them and to take better care of them in future.

Forgiveness

'If we really want to love, we must learn how to forgive.'
MOTHER TERESA, SAINT

Forgiving others

The following exercise has been adapted from the process-based model of forgiveness authored by Robert Enright, PhD, one of the world's leading forgiveness researchers, and the Human Development Study Group,[1] and may help you understand whom to forgive and how to do it. Intervention testing of the model has had beneficial effects.[2] If you feel you'd benefit from forgiving someone and removing that heavy baggage from your shoulders, why not give it a go?

Exercise: Forgiving others

- List people who you feel have hurt you deeply enough to warrant forgiveness.
- Order them from those who have hurt you least to those who have hurt you the most.
- Start with the least. Recall how they came to hurt you and how that impacted your life. Allow any negative emotions to arise.
- Be mindful to contain the pain rather than dumping it back on the person who hurt you or on loved ones or friends.
- When you feel ready, make the decision to forgive the person.
- Ask yourself questions about them. What was life like for them as a child, then growing up? What wounds have they suffered? Was there additional stress in their life at the time they hurt you? These questions are not to excuse their behaviour, but they may help you understand them better.
- Notice if you feel any small sense of compassion towards the person who hurt you. Perhaps you've acknowledged they regret their actions or felt confused or misguided. Are your feelings becoming softer towards them?
- Symbolize the forgiveness with a gift for the person, perhaps in the form of a kind word about them, a smile, a phone call or a note in your journal. Keep your safety a priority.

- Complete the forgiveness process by finding meaning in your experience. Perhaps you're now more sensitive to the pain of others, especially those who have experienced something similar to you, and feel moved to help them.
- Now carry on with your list until you've forgiven the person who hurt you the most.

Note: Forgiveness doesn't excuse the behaviour or require you to forget what happened. It's not a reconciliation negotiated between the two of you, unless you wish it to be. Not everyone is meant to be in your future; some just pass through your life to teach you valuable lessons.

Forgiving yourself

> *'You can't start the next chapter of your life if you keep re-reading the last one.'*
> ANONYMOUS

I find the reason most people struggle to communicate with animals is because they feel guilty over something to do with their own animals. Often this is the manner of their death and whether they did or didn't do something right – 'right' being very subjective. Guardians will often get stuck in the belief that they let their animal down.

I've learned animals don't bear grudges. The most common view is that they know we humans have done the best we can with the skills and information we had, and even if that's not entirely the truth, animals seem to have a better understanding of life and death than we do, seeing it more like a circle without a start or end point.

Why is self-forgiveness so important?

If we don't allocate time for self-forgiveness, we hold on to our guilt and it halts the possibility of our being the best version of ourselves. Instead, we choose to live life in a state of fear or worry.

The path to forgiveness is not an easy one, especially when it's yourself you're trying to forgive, but if you don't take it:

- You get locked in the past and are unable to move on.
- You prevent yourself from achieving your goals.
- You prevent yourself from living a positive and fulfilling life.
- You prevent yourself from learning and improving from your mistakes.

Here's a simple exercise to help you:

Exercise: Self-forgiveness

- *Diagnose:* Identify why you need to forgive yourself.
- *No one is perfect:* Don't think that failing at something makes you a terrible person.

- *Start over:* Learning to forgive yourself is about learning to live with the past and learning from that experience. Don't dwell on the past; bring your focus to the present. Let the past be in the past.
- *Create a new mindset:* Learn from past mistakes and learn to be mindful. Be kinder to yourself, because knowledge and growth come from the experience of life.

When you can tell your story and it doesn't make you cry, that's when you know you've healed.

Self-care

Make your own self-care list

> *'Self-preservation is the first law of nature.'*
> ENGLISH PROVERB

Caring for yourself is one of the most important things you can do. It's also one of the easiest to forget. When we spend time helping and caring for others, it's easy to neglect our own needs. Very soon we're feeling run down and worn out. It's like running on empty. We need to recharge.

When we help ourselves first, then we can be more effective at helping others, both humans and animals. The great news is that practising self-care doesn't have to cost that much. It can even be free. I invite you to write your own self-care plan.

Exercise: Make your own self-care list

Here are some of the things on mine:

- Walks in nature.
- Quiet time alone.
- Sit outside and listen to the birdsong.
- Silly time – watching a film like *Paddington 2* (loved it!) or having a silly moment. The inner child needs fun too.
- Healthy eating – I've worked out my body loves green food.
- Talk openly with a trusted friend.
- Off the butt time – Pilates, yoga, badminton.
- Dream time – daydreaming can lead to bright ideas.
- Listening to music.
- Hot bath with magnesium bath flakes.
- Meditation.
- Buying beautiful flowers to admire.
- Face pampering, a massage or spa day.
- Buying a new journal for processing, self-reflection and inspirational ideas.
- Sleep. Sleep. Sleep. More sleep!
- Champagne o'clock – it would be unbalanced to be too virtuous.

Psst! Every time you improve yourself, it improves those around you too.

Ten things to scratch from your worry list

> *'Be a warrior, not a worrier.'*
>
> ANONYMOUS

I find that students who lean towards fear rather than trust do struggle with animal communication. Worry is a way of thinking, a pattern of behaviour. It can also be a coping mechanism.

A study conducted by Dr Cavert and financed by America's National Science Foundation discovered that people expend 92 per cent of their emotional energy being concerned about things that won't happen or things they can't change.[3] That's a lot of energy gone to waste.

The good news is that worry can be transformed, but it takes a little effort. The essential ingredients of transforming worry are:

- *Breaking the habit:* You can do this by finding a way of staying present in the moment, not concerned about the future or past or what may or may not be.
- *Trusting in life:* Accept you're not in control. Instead trust in the flow of life and everything working out for the highest good.
- *Releasing your past:* If you hold on to fear, resentment and regret, these frequencies will be vibrating in your body. This is draining for you and tiring for the

animals in your life. It's time to let go for everyone's wellbeing.

Exercise: Ten things to scratch from your worry list

If you feel that you might benefit from releasing some of your worries, try this exercise:

- Write down 10 things you're worrying about. For example, 'I worry I will never be able to communicate with my cat.'
- With your hands on your heart say to yourself, 'I surrender fear and trust all will be well.'
- Scratch out each worry by drawing a line through it.
- Set fire to the worry list (safely) and watch all of your fears transform to ashes, or rip them to pieces if you prefer. Symbolism is very powerful.
- Affirm this transformation by saying out loud, '*Hakuna Matata*!' It's a Swahili phrase that roughly translates to 'No worries' and it's also the title of a song from *The Lion King* musical. And it's fun!
- Reflect: Notice how it feels to have a body vibrating with the energy of trust now that all of the draining energies of worry have been released.

Tip: If you feel you need more help, look into the Emotional Freedom Technique (EFT) or other healing modalities until you find one that works for you.

Waterfall cleansing

Water is a great cleanser and conduit for releasing blockages and letting go of feelings that no longer serve you.

Meditation: Waterfall cleansing

Find a quiet place. Relax, ground yourself and breathe in stillness.

Now find yourself outside in nature, surrounded by rolling hills, lakes and mountains.

You hear the sounds of the mountain birds.

You become aware of animals going about their business.

You feel the warm sunshine on your skin.

And notice the cloudless blue sky.

A huge mountain is close by and you walk over to the foot of it.

You notice a path that winds up towards the top.

Start walking up that winding path.

As you climb higher, you begin to notice the weight on your shoulders and the heaviness of the burdens that you're carrying on your back. You become aware of tiredness, resentment, anger or pain. With each step you find the climb is harder and slower.

You continue step by step with the knowledge of all the burdens you are carrying, burdens that you had not even realized you'd asked for, but are with you anyway.

You feel hot, sweaty and exhausted by the weight of emotions and blocks that you are hanging on to. You wish to rest. You wish to be free of these burdens.

Then you notice a small opening ahead of you and the most beautiful azure blue waterfall comes into sight.

The spray of gushing water sparkles and glistens in the beams of sunlight. Birds are singing a joyful song and dancing in the air. There is a warm, welcoming feeling that beckons you closer. This feels like a magical place, full of wonder, full of light.

Without hesitation, you remove your clothes and walk over to the waterfall. You feel lighter already, just by being close to it.

You step underneath it and feel the cooling water falling down on you.

Glittering and iridescent, the water starts to cleanse you. Thousands of little stars rain down on you. You feel the heaviness of your burdens being washed away. You see them as chunks of darkness being dissolved in the vibration of love.

With each minute, you feel lighter and more blissful. All your sadness, all your fear, all your guilt, is being gently cleansed away.

You start to feel what it's like to live without the weight of those burdens.

You start to feel love for yourself and for others.

Spend as long as you wish under the soft caress of the waterfall, feeling her nurturing arms around you. You are completely safe, completely loved.

When you're ready, step out into the sun's warm rays and allow her to dry your skin. You feel refreshed and blessed.

Allow the sun to beam light into your body, into every organ, every bone, every muscle and every cell.

You feel strong.

Honour your naked body, your light, your love.

You feel more alive. You feel wonderful. Amazing.

When you're ready, you dress yourself, then make your way back down the path, noticing that you feel very different – relaxed, renewed, refreshed.

You may need to repeat this meditation a number of times or whenever you feel blocked. Every time it's repeated, you'll be releasing blockages and becoming clearer.

Stop self-sabotaging

> *'It's better to regret what you have done than what you haven't.'*
> Paul Arden, author

Do you have a negative voice in your head that never stops putting you down? 'You'll never be able to communicate with animals,' it says. 'How do you know that's right? You're just making it up.' This is the voice of your inner critic. No wonder it's hard to muster confidence and self-esteem in the face of this assault.

The purpose of the inner critic is to get you to fit in with the rules of your family, society and culture. The inner critic wants you to be accepted. But it also wants you to obey without question. And if you wish to communicate with animals, you need to break some societal rules right off the bat, possibly including the rules of your family and culture. My parents thought I was crazy leaving a successful career in which I'd established a great reputation to go and do something they didn't value; they had no form of reference for animal communication and just didn't get it.

Not everyone's with the programme. And that's okay.

The problem comes when you feel you don't fit in and the inner critic is trying to get you to do just that. It's impossible to live up to the expectations and rules of the inner critic, which in turn can leave you feeling anxious that you're never good enough.

If you're feeling like this, just *stop*. You *are* good enough. If you've been called a maverick or nonconformist, or unconventional or eccentric, then woo-hoo, you're streets ahead. You're going to find entering the wonderful world of animal communication much easier than those who toe the line.

I've always followed my passion, even if it's seemed bonkers to those around me at the time. My approach is that I'd rather try and fail than never try at all. Life's too short to be following someone else's rules and life plan.

Two words I strive to eradicate from my vocabulary, workshop room and home are 'should' and 'shouldn't'. The inner critic loves these words, because of their power. They can make us give up and stop trying in a heartbeat. They can also get us to do something that our heart doesn't want to do, out of the pressure of convention and fitting in.

Try eliminating 'should' or 'shouldn't' from your vocab for a month.

Procrastination is another form of self-sabotaging, and people with low self-esteem are more likely to sabotage themselves when something good happens to them, because they don't feel deserving. Let's look at that next.

Restore self-esteem

> *'You are free. You are powerful. You are good. You are love. You have value. You have a purpose. All is well.'*
>
> ABRAHAM-HICKS, INSPIRATIONAL SPEAKER

To overcome self-sabotaging behaviour, learn to separate from your inner critic and transform it into a friend rather than an enemy. Do this by hearing its voice and working out the rules it's trying to enforce. Evaluate those rules and see if they hold any validity. For instance, 'You're never going to do it.' How does the voice know? You haven't even tried yet. A response could be, 'No, that's not true. I haven't even tried and I want to give it a go.'

Repeat this method whenever the critic chirps up and over time you'll notice the voice is turning from a negative naysayer into a faithful friend. By taking charge of the negative voice, handling it assertively and befriending it, any underlying vulnerabilities that fuel its fire will be extinguished. You'll be able to live a more empowered and stress-free life with greater confidence and increased self-esteem. Now we're cooking with gas!

Confidence doesn't mean that you're always right, by the way; it means that you're not afraid to be wrong. But it's better to live with remorse than regrets.

'I am…'

> *'I'm not normal. I don't want to be. I don't pretend to be. I am me.'*
>
> Anonymous

We have to be careful whenever we declare, 'I am…' because that can all too easily become our truth. For example, 'I am rubbish at running.' Yet if I practised and took on a coach, I'd improve no end. So it's not true.

The aim is to reach a point, shadow side and all, where you go, 'I am perfect just the way I am.' That's not an egoist statement. You can declare yourself perfect, warts and all. You're basically confirming: '*I love myself no matter what*.'

One 'I am' statement I particularly like is: 'I am love.' I'm sure you can create ones that resonate with you. Or adopt mine, if you like it. I'm sharing.

Let go for serenity

One of the stories in my first book, *Heart to Heart: Incredible and heartwarming stories from the woman who talks with animals*, is about a python called Ruby who taught me that I didn't need to hold fear. Many people fear snakes, as I did, without having encountered one. It would be more logical to be fearful of mosquitos and contracting malaria. When I first held Ruby, in my very first skin to scales experience, I was scared. She taught me to let go of that fear. The fear I held inside myself that had nothing to do with what she was doing. She was calm and peaceful in my hands.

This royal python taught all the humans present how emotional and caring snakes can be when they are really seen for themselves. She taught us all that our fear of snakes was in fact a reflection of our own fear.

She helped us to let go of that fear by expressing deep love and by repeating the phrase 'Let go.' I found myself moving from a vibration of fear into one of serenity.

If you're holding any fear, I hope Ruby's story and these affirmations will help you to release it:

'I let go of my fear.'

'I let go of all my fearful thoughts.'

'I let go and release fear.'

'I let go and transform fear.'

'I let go and surrender.'

'I let go and find peace.'

'I let go and find love.'

'I let go and I am love.'

Meet your inner dolphin

> *'If joy could talk, this is what she would say. It was Love that gave birth to me.'*
>
> Rumi, poet

This meditation is a great way to lift your mood and empower yourself through play. It's fantastic to connect with dolphin energy because it's so joyful and fun.

Meditation: Meet your inner dolphin

Find a quiet place and lie down.

Relax, ground and still yourself.

Surrender to silence.

Release your muscles.

And breathe.

Bring your awareness into your heart and connect with love.

Visualize your heart's love expanding, beaming soft pink rays of love outwards and all around you.

You become aware of an image of a tiny dolphin far away in the distance, leaping and spinning.

As you focus on the dolphin it becomes larger and larger. Growing in size, it's coming closer and closer to you.

You can feel its immense happiness.

The dolphin comes even closer to you now. You can see its beak and famous smile. You can see its tail fluke, pectoral and dorsal fins.

The dolphin is sharing so much joy with you. It's infectious. You feel the dolphin joy transmitting to every part of you – every organ, every muscle, every atom of your being.

The joy brings lightness with it. You start to feel lighter and lighter as you increase in joy.

So close now, you look directly into the face of your dolphin.

You have eye-to-eye contact.

It is as if time has stopped.

You are seen. As if you were completely naked.

You feel held and recognized.

The dolphin knows you. And you know the dolphin. You are old friends reunited – back together in love.

You feel so much joy in your heart, it ripples through you.

You feel at one with your dolphin.

Family. Pod. Oneness.

It's now time for play. See yourself in the turquoise blue ocean, able to breathe underwater.

Your dolphin invites you to play with them. Together you swim and spin and dive deep then leap joyfully out of the water.

You dive deep again, racing towards a leaf, seeing who will reach it first.

Your dolphin does, but then drops it for you to chase it. You reach for it, and just as you do, the dolphin whizzes past and takes it on its pectoral fin. What fun!

The dolphin swims around you, nodding their head, inviting more play.

This time you take the leaf and drop it. Your dolphin comes zooming in to retrieve it, then passes it back to you to drop it again.

You continue to play, and dive, and leap, and spin, enjoying the joy, enjoying the fun, enjoying the play.

Thank your dolphin for this special time. And for reminding you just how important it is to give time to play. How much joy there can be having fun for fun's sake. And how important it is for you to step away from routines, responsibility and rules.

Your dolphin has a name. Say to them, 'Please share your name with me. What do you like to be called?' This way, whenever you wish to be with them again, in this joy, in this love, feeling playful, having fun, they will hear your call and come close.

Receive your dolphin's name and thank them.

Say goodbye to your dolphin now, leave them playing in the ocean and bring your awareness to land, back to your body, where you are lying down.

Recall your memory of playing with your inner dolphin. Notice how it made you feel and how you feel now – somewhat lighter, freer, more joyful.

Express gratitude for this experience and know you can play with your inner dolphin as often as you like.

When you're ready, bring your awareness back to your environment, back to your body, your fingers and toes.

Take a gentle breath.

And when you're ready, open your eyes.

Stewart's advice

> *'Enlightenment is when a wave realizes it is the ocean.'*
>
> Thich Nhat Hanh, monk

I'd like to end this chapter by sharing some advice from a wise Maine Coon called Stewart. He has now transitioned, but I was lucky to meet him, and his guardians, when he was still in physical form. Stewart and his guardians happily agreed to share his teachings with you.

Teaching #1

Ask not, 'What should I be doing?' but 'What will make me happy?' Follow this direction with all your heart, and your soul will fly free and soar.

Teaching #2

Raise your eyes now. Listen to the birds, the trees, the sun, the Earth. These have qualities you need. The qualities will raise your vibration and life will seem easy once more.

Teaching #3

There are three things I advise you to change.

1. *Your breath*: Breathe more deeply to connect with energy.

2. *Your outlook*: Only think positive thoughts.
3. *Your agenda*: Follow your heart on all matters.

Thank you, Stewart.

SUMMARY

- Challenges are boulders you can transform into stepping stones to growth and success.
- Remember your three 'P's: practice, patience and persistence.
- The ABC of animal communication: Adjust your attitude, Beware biology, Cultivate compassion.
- Make self-care your number one priority.
- Release worry and be a warrior.
- Cleanse yourself of anything that no longer serves you.
- Connect with your inner dolphin joy.

Chapter 8

What's Next for You?

'The greatness of a nation and its moral progress can be judged by the way its animals are treated.'

MAHATMA GANDHI, ACTIVIST

I've shared with you the first steps and provided you with the tools to help you develop. You now need to practise animal communication and engage with self-development. Once you've got to grips with the basic steps, are learning to manage self-doubt, and are spending more time in trust and flow, you'll probably feel ready to expand your knowledge.

The creatures in your garden

When you've completed eight or more communications and start to feel quite confident, you can start reaching out to the creatures in your garden or vicinity. Verification may be nigh on impossible with them, but you can have fun.

Exercise: Birds and insects communicate too

Approach this lightly and as an exercise to dissolve limited thinking and get out of the box.

Use the same five-step method of preparation and communication, then ask the birds and insects around you questions you believe they'll find interesting. For example:

- 'What does it feel like to sing?'
- 'Where do you sleep?'
- 'What foods do you love eating?'
- 'What do you enjoy doing?'
- 'Do you have a message you'd like to share with humans?'
- 'Do you have any advice on how I can improve my animal communication?'

Go with the first impressions you receive, write them down and try and have a telepathic conversation based on the animal's responses. Practise for just a few minutes at a time and build slowly to more lengthy conversations. Always end with the ritual of disconnection (*see page 126*).

Intermediate subjects

The next natural progression for you would be to explore the 'intermediate' subjects of body scanning, Gestalt and remote viewing. I'll touch on them lightly here.

Body scanning

This is when you learn how to sense and receive information about how the animal's body feels using your eyes like an airport scanner. Hence the term 'body scan'.

Gestalt

This is when you learn how to move your awareness from your own body and into an animal's body. It's a bit like leaving land and entering a submarine to explore unknown deep ocean territory. Okay, it's not like that, but you might know what I mean...

Remote viewing

You'll have heard the term, but may not have realized it's also a skill used within animal communication. It's the practice of seeking impressions – images, sensations, colours, textures, smells, size, etc. – about a distant or unseen target.

Tracking missing animals

Remote viewing is most useful when learning how to track a missing animal and is best paired with the Gestalt method, as well as the basic communication skills you've learned from this book. Utilizing all of the skills, rather than relying solely on one, gives you the best chance of understanding where your animal is, whether they are still in their body or transitioned, and, if possible, how you may be reunited with them.

I offer intermediate workshops in these three skill methods for when you're ready to take your animal communication further. There are some great examples of when I've found missing animals using these skills in my first book, *Heart to Heart*, including two separate cases where the dogs were trapped underground.

If your animal goes missing, I offer a free 'Lost Animal' guide on my website, which can help you, and it includes the visualizations I share with clients. Tracking is the hardest skill and it's very complex, so don't beat yourself up if you struggle with this one. Please do try and communicate with your own animal to find them, but, as it will be a very emotional time, I suggest you consult a professional animal communicator if you need further support.

Developing your sensitivity to energy

There are so many ways to do this and tons of books on it, so I'll just share a few that have worked well for me.

Reiki

Early on I felt Morgan guiding me to learn Reiki and I'm now a Usui Reiki Master. Reiki is a form of alternative medicine developed in 1922 by Japanese Buddhist Mikao Usui. It's a natural healing system that anyone can benefit from and it works on every level: physical, spiritual, mental and emotional. It helps you increase your sensitivity to force energy and is also a healing modality that you can use for yourself and your animals. A win-win!

Psychic or intuitive development

When I first attended animal communication workshops, I heard terms I didn't fully understand, so I attended the College of Psychic Studies in London to explore subjects like chakras and auras. If they interest you, you might find there's a group near you or an online course that will help you gain more knowledge about these areas. Things went full circle when I was invited to be a visiting teacher at the college and began teaching animal communication there. It's funny where life takes us.

Meditation classes

If you struggle to be present or to quieten your mind, some regular classes in meditation could be just what you need to get into the habit. Guided meditations can also help you understand yourself on a deeper level. Sometimes these things are easier in a group and you get to meet like-minded people and exchange mutual support. There are so many different types of meditation for you to try.

Beneficial practices

Gong baths

Personally, I adore these. I find them very cleansing and healing. They can also help remove blockages. Contrary to the title, you don't get into a bath and get wet. You tend to be lying down and someone will tap a gong and the sound will wash over you and through you, bathing you in the sound.

Having had a few gong baths, I've found some people are more skilled at it than others, so if you don't like it the first time, do try it again with someone else, as not all gong baths are the same.

An altar

It's nice to have a designated sacred place with things that have great meaning to you, like photographs of your animals, pebbles or crystals, leaves or feathers. It's a place of focus and harmony and you can also sit in front of it to meditate or communicate.

Rituals

A ritual is a symbolic event that helps to solidify an internal event. It can be as simple as lighting a candle or incense, making specific movements, singing or toning, grouping objects together, a way of dressing, a mantra, dancing, or using an object as part of your ritual practice. Whatever it is, it is performed with care and thought. Have a clear purpose and reasons for doing it before you begin.

Think about creating a personal ritual before you communicate with an animal. For example, I perform a ritual, carry out a routine you could say, before every workshop I teach. I sit by myself in the room, cleanse the space with reiki and sometimes incense, offer a blessing, invite animals in to support the day and ask for guidance. I also place photographs of my animals beside me.

More advanced areas of animal communication

Animal loss

If you love sharing your life with animals, at some point it's inevitable that you're going to experience animal loss. It can be devastating for some, even more traumatic than the loss of a parental figure, sibling or close friend, such is the power of the unconditional love animals give. After an animal's death, it's human for us to question, 'Did I do it right?', 'What happens to animals when they die?' and 'Will they come back to me?' We often feel immense grief that is made much harder by a society that largely invalidates grief for animals.

This subject is so important to Morgan and me that we wrote a book about it called *The Animal Communicator's Guide Through Life, Loss and Love*. If you're offering palliative care, facing loss or grieving for a loved one, then I recommend this book as a means to support you. It's also helpful if you're caring for another person who's grieving for their animal. I offer a workshop on this too, called 'Life, Loss and Love'.

Reincarnation

Again, this is a huge subject and animals offer their perspective on it in 'Life, Loss and Love'. I have communicated with many animals who have passed over and relayed their messages back to their guardians. Some have chosen to stay on the other side, reincarnate elsewhere or been undecided, and a very small number have decided to return, in some form, to the human they've just left. Why? Well, that's another book.

One more thing I want to share which may help you is that I categorically couldn't give a fig to the notion that there is one heaven for humans and a separate heaven for animals. Balderdash! Humans are made up of water, oxygen and empty space. We're just like other animals in the animal kingdom. The belief that there is a hierarchy, once we shed our physical shell and return to dust, is one that originates from ego and superiority.

Animals as our healers and teachers

This is another huge subject. Animals change human lives, but have you ever stopped to ask why? I believe one of the many things that draw us to animals is that they have the capacity to deliver powerful lessons in gentle, loving ways. Plenty of people have shared with me the profound impact their animals have had on them. Animals have even saved lives. Guardians have revealed that when they have been contemplating ending their lives, their animal friends have been able to pull them out of that dark despair.

Sometimes animals keep us going in obvious ways: we need to get up in the morning to feed or walk them. But there are also other ways: it's how they lean into us, look into our eyes, place a paw on our body, perch on our shoulder or clown around to make us laugh that heals our heart and helps *make life a much better place to be*. Some cats will drape their body across our heart area and purr. Some dogs will lick away our salty tears and gently rest their head in our lap (like in the book and film *Marley and Me*).[1] Horses will drop their head and 'hold' us in a hug. Animals have an ability to express great compassion and kindness to the humans they care about, and sometimes strangers too.

Another reason we love animals so much is that they 'see' us. They know us. They see past the veils we draw over ourselves and connect with us deeply – to our thoughts, feelings and anxieties. And, despite seeing and knowing us, *animals accept us*. Being accepted seems to be very important to humans. It's a validation that we're okay. Or, in simpler terms, it's the 'I love you' that we long for. Because one of the human conditions is anxiety, we find it challenging to provide ourselves with this sense of acceptance and unconditional love.

Animals also heal us by getting us to become more aware of and connected with nature. If you walk your dog or go out with your horse, you gain insight into the sounds and smells of the world around you. You see the beauty of dew on a spider's web.

In short, animals teach us to:

- play
- trust
- love
- be balanced
- be in the moment
- lighten up
- forgive quickly
- be joyful
- enhance our relationship with the natural world
- respect ourselves and others

Guides and power animals

Animals can also be our spiritual teachers. You can progress to learn how to recognize your guides and 'power animals' and communicate with them. I teach a workshop on this called 'Empowering Animals', because that's ultimately what these animals do – they empower us. They can be the animals in our lives, but also the animals we've loved who have passed over, and other species too, like ants, robins, sheep or wombats.

Wild animal wisdom

Annually, I take people on international wild animal communication retreats where they learn how to communicate with animals they may never have encountered – species like dolphins, humpback whales, sea turtles, manta rays, grizzly bears and orcas. These natural habitat experiences give people an amazing opportunity to form deep connections with wild animals and to receive their wisdom and guidance through communication.

In return, the animals are aware they're raising awareness about their species and that the humans they teach will be the animal ambassadors of the future, talking respectfully and compassionately about their species and generating a ripple effect across humanity.

These wild animal retreats are profoundly transformative experiences. There are participants who value them so much they attend every retreat I facilitate.

Rise and sparkle

'Kindness is free. Sprinkle that stuff everywhere.'
Anonymous

There is a shift happening in human consciousness, and people have a desire to become more connected and aware. Those who love animals are meeting that desire by creating even closer connections with them. The interest in animal communication has skyrocketed since I first discovered it in 2004.

Animals also take us out into nature and open our hearts to the environment, where we come to recognize our role as custodians with an individual responsibility to care for and preserve Mother Earth and all who inhabit her. When you witness with your own eyes the impact of human choices on wildlife and the planet, apathy is no longer a viable option.

The sharks know

'Life on Earth depends on life in the ocean.'
Rob Stewart, conservationist

Sharks have been here more than 400 million years – that's 100 million years *before* the dinosaurs, when life had only just begun on land. We now know that life evolved from the sea. The first animals were tiny single-cell organisms that gave rise to algae, coral and tiny planktonic animals. The ocean is basically the life support of the planet, down to the very smallest plankton upon which all life relies, and, as Dr Boris Worm, a marine conservation biologist, said, 'We know that predators are fundamentally controlling the structure and functioning of the ecosystems.'[2] In the oceans, that means sharks.

An American politician has declared a hatred of sharks, perhaps because a) he's unaware that soda pop machines kill more people than sharks do; b) he's unaware sharks hold life in balance and are one of the species we humans can't live without.

> *Deaths caused to humans annually by: sharks 8; road accidents: 1,200,000; starvation: 8,000,000.*[3]

Did you know that humans are 75 times more likely to be killed by lightning than a shark? But it's very different when humans kill sharks:

> *Deaths caused to sharks by humans annually: 100,000,000 (more likely 273 million). Humans kill 11,417 sharks per hour.*[4]

And finally, a quiz question:

> *Question: Which species is the only one to remain unchanged in 400 million years and to have also survived the five major extinctions that have wiped most life from the planet?*
>
> *Answer: Sharks.*

Clearly, sharks know more than we do. Grab a copy of the eye-opening documentary *Sharkwater* by Rob Stewart.[5]

Our planet is showing us, with her demonstrations of storms, heatwaves, floods, droughts and wild fires, that we need to become more compassionate and caring as a species. According to the National Climate Assessment, 'Human influences are the number one cause of global warming,'[6] and evidence shows that '2000 to 2009 was hotter than any other decade in at least the past *1,300 years*.'[7] The ice is melting. The ocean is filling with plastic, noise pollution and toxins. Non-human species are going extinct because of what we're doing. It's vital we remember that our own species is reliant on all the other species for existence. It's time we put caring into action. It's the best way to overcome despair.

The future is the compassionate heart

> *'Whatever the question, Love is the answer.'*
>
> Dr Wayne W. Dyer, philosopher

You're probably wondering what global warming and species extinction have to do with animal communication. The answer is *everything*. It's all interconnected, and animals don't only communicate about what they want to eat and what they feel about the new dog walker, they care about the planet. Domestic animals, garden wildlife, zoo animals and wild animals living in their natural habitat all have an awareness of the damage being done to the natural world. They care about their own and other species, and they would like us to care too.

Animals want us to put love into action

> *'We are called to be people of conviction, not conformity; of moral nobility, not social respectability.'*
>
> Martin Luther King, minister

I believe this is a reason why animal communication is taking off as fast as it is right now. It's not new – people have being communicating with animals for centuries – but now it's needed more than ever. Not so that Fluffykins can have the cat bed of her dreams and a diamante tiara, but so that the non-human animals can reconnect *us* to *our* hearts and encourage us to be more compassionate-led beings.

We have become so egocentric as a species that we think we're the centre of the universe and the universe revolves around us. Admittedly we are part of the universe – and every time we accept a plastic straw, use a plastic cotton bud, accept a plastic bag or purchase fish caught through long lining, we are contributing to the extinction of species and impacting the balance of the ecosystem that sustains our own lives.

As technology gets faster and the new is replaced by the newer, we are sidetracked by our consumer greed, egocentric nature and lack of self-worth to believe that all of the answers in life revolve around *things*. In a way, they do: what we consume matters. Primatologist Jane Goodall reminds us that we are all consumers: 'By exercising free choice, by choosing what to buy, what not to buy, we have the power, collectively, to change the ethics of business, of industry. We have the potential to exert immense power for good.'[8]

It's time to snap out of denial and laziness. We need to understand and embody that we are part of the same environment and make conscious choices. We must stop leaving it to 'them' out there and take individual responsibility. These are responsibilities that come with growing into an animal communicator.

We are co-existing beings of consciousness

> *'Don't you know yet? It is your Light that lights up the world.'*
>
> Rumi, poet

I started this book talking about the wonders of technology. While technology is capable of extraordinary things, it can't connect us to our heart space, the compassionate self where we remember and explore our deepest connections with all living beings. Animals can help us re-establish our connection with the natural world and the spiritual power that exists in and all around us.

I believe animals are the gateway to a higher awareness of spirituality. Humans have created a mess of things; animals have the answer. By learning how to communicate with them, we can learn to become a more compassionate species, a caring species, with a role as the custodians and preservers of all life.

I invite you to be an ambassador for animals, to help raise awareness, to listen to the animals' wise guidance and to be a part of the positive ripple effect of sharing the truth of animal sentience from the core of your compassionate heart.

A compassionate world starts with you. Put love into action.

Allow me to end this book with a blessing for all animal species.

The animal blessing

May all beings be happy.

May all beings be free.

May all beings know joy.

May all beings know love.

You are Loved.

You are Love.

I am Love.

We are Love.

You and I,

We are Love.

As Love

Are we.

SUMMARY

- Your next subjects can include body scanning, Gestalt and remote viewing.
- Develop further with the help of Reiki, psychic or intuitive development and meditation.
- Beneficial practices can include gong baths, creating an altar and performing rituals.
- More advanced subjects can include animal loss, reincarnation, animals as our healers and teachers, guides and power animals, and wild animal wisdom.
- A compassionate world starts with you. Put love into action.

Ethics and Practice Guidelines

These ethics are for beginners in animal communication and are adapted from Penelope Smith's 'Code of Ethics for Interspecies Communicators'.[1]

- Our motivation is compassion for all beings and a desire to help all species understand each other better, particularly to help restore the lost human ability to freely and directly communicate with other species.
- We honour those who come to us for help, not judging, condemning or invalidating them for their mistakes or misunderstanding, but honouring their desire for change and harmony.
- We know that to keep this work as pure and harmonious as possible requires that we continually grow spiritually.
- We realize that telepathic communication can be clouded or overlaid by our own unfulfilled emotions,

critical judgements or lack of love for ourselves and others.

- We walk in humility, willing to recognize and clear up our own errors in understanding others' communication (human and non-human alike).
- We get whatever education and/or personal help we need to do our work effectively, with compassion, respect, joy and harmony.
- We seek to draw out the best in everyone.
- We go only where we are asked to help, so that others are receptive and we truly can help.
- We respect the feelings and ideas of others and work for interspecies understanding.
- We acknowledge the things that we cannot change and continue where we can be most effective.
- We respect the privacy of the people and animal companions we communicate with, and honour their desire for confidentiality.
- While doing our best to help, we allow others their own dignity and help them to help their animal companions.
- We cultivate understanding and ability in others, rather than dependence on our ability.
- We offer people ways to be involved in understanding and growth with their fellow beings of other species.

- We acknowledge our limitations and seek help from other professionals as needed. It is not our job to name and treat diseases, and we refer people to veterinarians for the diagnosis of physical illness.
- We may relay animals' ideas, feelings, pains and symptoms as they describe them or as we feel or perceive them, and this may be helpful to veterinary health professionals.
- The goal of any interspecies experience is more communication, balance, compassion, understanding and communion among all beings.
- We follow our heart, honouring the spirit and life of all beings as One.

Practice guidelines

Manage expectations

When requesting case studies for practice, begin by being transparent that i) you're new to animal communication and may not always be correct; ii) the information is for verification purposes; and iii) the animal's guardian must be discerning about the animal's wellbeing.

Respect the animal

When you practise, it can be very easy to forget that this isn't just about you improving; primarily and always, it's about the animal. Show them the respect they deserve and if they're not interested in helping you, walk away.

Respect the guardian

Whenever you're practising, remember you still have a responsibility to empower the guardian and not to undermine or belittle their efforts based on their current knowledge or means.

Remember your responsibility

Winston Churchill said, 'The price of greatness is responsibility.' When communicating with your own or friends' animals for case studies, keep your focus on developing greater understanding between species and the highest good of the animal. Animal communication must never be used as a method of control.

Be an animal communication ambassador

Even when starting out, you still have a role as an animal communication ambassador, representing animal communication in its truest, most ethical and compassionate form. Be mindful not to jeopardize its reputation and the reputation of all who practise it ethically with love and compassion, through selfish gain or misguided methods.

References

Chapter 1: Overview of Animal Mommunication

1. https://www.survivalinternational.org/tribes/aboriginals
2. The Cambridge Declaration on Consciousness: http://fcmconference.org/img/CambridgeDeclarationOnConsciousness.pdf

Chapter 2: Shifting Perspective

1. Phillip Hamrick, Jarrad A. G. Lum and Michael T. Ullman, 'Child first language and adult second language are both tied to general-purpose learning systems', *Proceedings of the National Academy of Sciences*, Jan. 2018, 201713975; DOI: 10.1073/pnas.1713975115; http://www.pnas.org/content/early/2018/01/25/1713975115
2. Rupert Sheldrake, *Dogs That Know When Their Owners Are Coming Home: And other unexplained powers of animals*, Hutchinson, 1999; new edition, Arrow, 2011
3. Mark Leary, 'Don't beat yourself up: learning to be kind to yourself when you inevitably make mistakes could have a remarkable effect on your happiness', https://aeon.co/essays/learning-to-be-kind-to-yourself-has-remarkable-benefits
4. Abraham Tesser, Department of Psychology, University of Georgia, Athens, Georgia, http://journals.sagepub.com/doi/pdf/10.1111/1467-8721.00117

5. Heidi A. Wayment, PhD, and Jack J. Bauer, PhD, *Transcending Self-Interest: Psychological explorations of the quiet ego*, American Psychological Association, 2008
6. Lynne McTaggart, *The Field: The quest for the secret force of the universe*, HarperCollins, 2001

Chapter 3: How Does It Work?

1. Sophy Burnham, *The Art of Intuition: Cultivating your inner wisdom*, Jeremy P. Tarcher/Penguin, 2011
2. Enhancing Intuitive Decision Making Through Implicit Learning programme: http://www.researchgate.net/publication/281503122_Enhancing_Intuitive_Decision_Making_Through_Implicit_Learning
3. C. G. Jung, http://www.cgjungpage.org
4. Virko Kask, http://www.perzonality.com
5. Michael D. Gershon, *The Second Brain: The scientific basis of gut instinct and a ground breaking new understanding of nervous disorders of the stomach and intestine*, HarperCollins, 1998
6. 'Reflecting on Another's Mind', https://www.uzh.ch/cmsssl/suz/dam/jcr:ffffffff-fad3-547b-ffff-ffffa698c225/10.4_miller_05.pdf, and Dr Christian Keysers, https://nin.nl/about-us/the-organisation/team/christian-keysers/
7. *Moment* app, http://inthemoment.io
8. Annette Bolte, Thomas Goschke, Julius Kuhl, 'Emotion and intuition: effects of positive and negative mood on implicit judgments of semantic coherence', *Psychological Science* 14(5), 416–42; http://journals.sagepub.com/doi/abs/10.1111/1467-9280.01456
9. We Love Elephants, https://www.youtube.com/watch?v=J9WW3QbOgQA
10. Elaine Thompson, Sound Therapy UK: http://www.soundtherapyuk.com

11. Dr Masaru Emoto's research: http://www.masaru-emoto.net/english/water-crystal.html
12. David R. Hawkins, MD, PhD, *Power vs Force: The hidden determinants of human behaviour*, Veritas Publishing, 1995; Hay House, 2014

Chapter 5: Making a Connection

1. Professor Marius Usher's research: https://www.zmescience.com/research/studies/decision-making-intuition-accurate-42433/

Chapter 6: Effective Steps to Communicating with Your Own Animals

1. The HeartMath Institute, 'Coherence: A State of Optimal Function'; https://www.heartmath.org/programs/emwave-self-regulation-technology-theoretical-basis/
2. The HeartMath Institute, 'The Heart and Emotions', https://www.heartmath.org/articles-of-the-heart/science-of-the-heart/the-energetic-heart-is-unfolding/
3. BBC series *Blue Planet 2*, https://www.amazon.co.uk/Blue-Planet-DVD-David-Attenborough/dp/B0758QDMC5
4. Cherokee legend, Two Wolves, http://www.firstpeople.us/FP-Html-Legends/TwoWolves-Cherokee.html

Chapter 7: Troubleshooting for Beginners

1. R.D. Enright and the Human Development Study Group, 'The Moral Development of Forgiveness' in W. Kurtines and J. Gewirtz (eds), *Handbook of Moral Behavior and development*, Vol. I, pp.123–52, Erlbaum, 1991
2. J.H. Hebl and R.D. Enright, 'Forgiveness as a psychotherapeutic goal with elderly females', *Psychotherapy* 30 (1993), 658–67
3. The National Science Foundation, https://www.nsf.gov

Chapter 8: What's Next for You?

1. John Grogan, *Marley and Me: Life and love with the world's worst dog*, William Morrow, 2005
2. Dr Boris Worm, http://wormlab.biology.dal.ca/project/global-marine-biodiversity-causes-consequences-conservation/
3. Human deaths by sharks: http://www.trackingsharks.com/2016-record-number-of-shark-attacks-bites/
4. Shark deaths by humans: http://www.greenpeace.org.au/blog/shark-attack/#.WnTJZrjeCRs
5. Rob Stewart, *Sharkwater*, SW Productions, Diatribe Pictures, Sharkwater Productions, 2006
6. The National Climate Assessment, https://nca2014.globalchange.gov/highlights/report-findings/our-changing-climate
7. The National Climate Assessment, https://www.nrdc.org/stories/are-effects-global-warming-really-bad
8. Dr Jane Goodall: http://www.janegoodall.org.uk

Ethics and Practice Guidelines

1. Penelope Smith, Anima Mundi Incorporated, https://www.animaltalk.net.

Resources

Suggested reading

Lawrence Anthony, *The Elephant Whisperer*, Sidgwick & Jackson, 2009

—, *The Last Rhinos*, Sidgwick & Jackson, 2012

J. Allen Boone, *Kinship with All Life*, Harper & Row, 2005

Jane Goodall, *Reason for Hope*, Grand Central Publishing, 1999

Allen M. Schoen, *Kindred Spirits*, Broadway Books, 2001

Lynne McTaggart, *The Field*, HarperCollins, 2001

Michael Talbot, *The Holographic Universe*, Grafton Books, 1991

Linda Tucker, *Saving the White Lions*, North Atlantic Books, 2013

Rosamund Young, *The Secret Life of Cows*, Faber and Faber, 2017

Films/documentaries

Jill Robinson: To the Moon and Back, dir. and writer, Andrew Tellinger, Orange Planet Pictures, 2017

Sharkwater, dir. and writer, Rob Stewart, SW Productions, Diatribe Pictures, Sharkwater Productions, 2006

Blackfish, Gabriela Couperthwaite, Eli Despres, Tim Zimmermann, dir. Gabriela Couperthwaite, Manny O Productions, 2013

The Cove, Mark Monroe, dir. Louie Psihoyos, Participant Media, 2009

Cowspiracy, dir. and writers, Kip Andersen, Keegan Kuhn, IndieGoGo, 2014

An Inconvenient Truth, Al Gore, dir. Davis Guggenheim, Lawrence Bender Productions, Participant Productions, 2006

Acknowledgements

Who is family? For me, it's those we resonate with the most. Without any advance evidence of success, their words are always 'Go for it', 'Follow your passion' or 'You must try, otherwise how will you ever know?' plus the all-important one: 'I believe in you.'

There's a woman in my life who has been cheering me on for over 20 years. Jo Town, thank you from the bottom of my heart for all of your love and encouragement on this journey.

Much love and thanks to my mother, Mary, who continues to believe in me and show me unconditional love.

Thank you to my tribe: Jane Hargreaves, Belinda Wright, Laura Scott and Roger Simonsz, fellow Podners and all the beautiful animal ambassadors across the world who join me hand in hand and heart to heart in the belief that together we can shake the world and make a difference to the lives of our glorious kindred spirits.

I also want to thank Texas, my co-author, for showing up at strategic times to put me back on track and to (occasionally) *tell* me what to write; Bodhi, my black dog friend, for his continued encouragement from the other side and support in writing this book; Morgan, who is never far away; and the divine Grace, a deep soul in the body of a beautiful dog, who has been one of the lucky ones to escape hardship in Romania and who is already teaching me so much about transmuting fear and anxiety frequencies into trust and love.

Thank you to my extended animal support team, power animals and to every animal I've had the honour of encountering, for teaching me so much. Thank you also to all the guardians who trust me with their animals when they need vital help. Thank you to every person who has ever attended my workshops, drawn there because of their love for animals. I am so grateful for the opportunity to share animal communication with you.

Sincere thanks also go to my commissioning editor, Amy Kiberd, editor and friend Lizzie Henry, and all the skilled people behind the scenes at Hay House UK who collaborate in making my words into a book you can hold in your hands, because our wish is for you to be inspired and empowered.

I wish to save my final thanks for you, the reader, for picking up this book, for entering into the world of animal communication, and for every communication you experience to help restore the deep relationship we have with animals and the natural world. Blessings to you. *Namaste*.

ABOUT THE AUTHOR

Pea Horsley is the UK's most highly regarded animal communicator. She is a TEDx speaker, grounded teacher, empowering mentor and the bestselling author of *Heart to Heart* and *The Animal Communicator's Guide Through Life, Loss and Love.*

Pea teaches internationally and has guided thousands of people to get back in touch with their intuition and develop skills in animal communication. She loves encouraging others to tap into their own intuitive knowing so their passions and dreams of being closer to animals can be made into reality.

Drawing on her childhood love and compassion for animals, Pea's passion is to bring deeper understanding and greater empathy towards other species and help people rekindle a profound connection with the natural world.

It's her great privilege to facilitate wild animal communication retreats for participants to experience face-to-face communication with wild animals in their natural habitat and learn from resident expert biologists. These retreats have included communicating with humpback whales, spinner dolphins, sea turtles, manta rays and pilot whales, to name just a few.

peahorsley

@peahorsley

www.animalthoughts.com